I0151635

LOVE IS LARGE

MAURICE & ROSE CHAVEZ

TABLE OF CONTENTS

Printed in the United States of America
First Printing, 2023

ISBN - 9781684188673

Maurice Chavez
Maurice.chavez68@gmail.com

I want to dedicate this book to my loving wife Rose, who has taught me to love in a LARGE way. She has loved me in ways that I cannot even begin to count and shown me love and patience. MUCH patience. She is the one person I know that loves everyone in a BIG way!

I also want to thank my daughters Jasmyn Munoz and Jadyn Chavez for loving me in a BIG way. These two remarkable young ladies are the life of why I love.

Also I want to thank my Granddaughter, Chloe, for showing me that LOVE is

INTRODUCTION

Two weeks before my wife and I were about to speak at a marriage retreat, we encountered some trials that literally forced us to learn this lesson. "Have you noticed that we always seem confronted by the things we teach?" my wife said. It wasn't something I had planned; it just happened that way. Obviously, God did not want us to teach from what we had not yet experienced. This was our norm.

My wife and I teach at marriage conferences and retreats. Since the mantle of marriage was passed on to us by our mentor, Dr. Leo Godzich, we felt the enormous weight of helping other couples experience the same life change that we had experienced. We didn't just want to impart a blanket teaching. We wanted men and women to leave, transformed so much that their marriages were reborn and revived.

Throughout our marriage, we have experienced the

tests of love. Through porn addiction and infidelity, we have faced the most destructive forces to marriage known, and some unknown, to man. We have literally learned what it means for our love to be large.

I met my wife when we were only sixteen and thirteen years of age. When we first met, it was not love at first sight, but God was working in ways we could not see. He orchestrated behind the scenes what we were to be. Every facet of our lives before and during our marriage has been carefully formed to help us become the best version of ourselves.

At the writing of this book, my wife and I have been together for twenty-nine years. We have not been with each other longer than either of us was with our parents. We have literally finished raising each other. I should say my wife has finished raising me. We have seen our lives go through more than hills and valleys. We have taken each other through Canyons and Crevasses. The pain we have brought to the marriage and inflicted on each other has taught us to trust God through our transformations.

It is in the process of molding and forming our marriage that we have learned the meaning of "Love is Large". We have learned to become the embodiment of patient love and the fruit of loving kindness. The bible verse found in 1 Corinthians 13:4-8 has always been one of my favorite verses, and I have quoted it often in marriage counseling and during marriage sermons. However, it wasn't until I heard the "Passion Bible Translation" that the verse became as vivid and colorful as a sunny day after a rainstorm.

⁴ Love is large and incredibly patient. Love is gentle and consistently kind to all. It refuses to be jealous when blessing comes to someone else. Love does not brag about one's achievements nor inflate its own importance. ⁵ Love does not traffic in shame and disrespect, nor selfishly seek its own honor. Love is not easily irritated or quick to take offense. ⁶ Love joyfully celebrates honesty and finds no delight in what is wrong. ⁷ Love is a safe place of shelter, for it never stops believing the best for others. Love never takes failure as defeat, for it never gives up. I Corinthians 13:4-8 TPT

Is Your Love Large Or Just Average?

The word large implies something is more than average. For your marriage to be what you have always dreamed, it should be that you will have to love in a way that is more than average. Average is plain pancakes with syrup. More than average pancakes have blue berries and bananas covered with melted butter and hot maple syrup. Average is a car with hand rolled windows and hand adjusted seats. A more than average car is the Q45 Infinity, with warmed seats, adjustable steering, heated cup holders, electronic seats that automatically adjust to its owner and electric windows. Do you get my point?

I think the reason we become so disappointed with our spouses is because we expect from them a more than average love when we are not investing a more than average love as well. We must be willing to love our spouses on a greater scale. Like kids who just bought their first Compact Disc and want to hear it on volume ten, we must ramp up our efforts to be a more than average husband or wife. We cannot expect to settle for mediocre and get next level results.

Jesus demonstrated His love for His bride in John 15:13 - *Greater love has no one than this: to lay down one's life for one's friends.* This is a classic demonstration of loving large. Average would have made conditions. Average would have set boundaries. Average would have expected returns.

Loving in an average way is like only cleaning the interior of your car, but not the outside. Loving large is like washing, waxing the exterior and detailing the interior, along with restoring the damage of tears and cracks in the vinyl. When someone loves in a large way, it is not loud to be noticed by others, but it is loving in a way that can be noticed by the one it is intended for.

Loving large is takes extreme measures to demonstrate the care for the other person. It is never selfish and self-centered when loving someone. Jesus in loving us, the church loved us even when we didn't love him. He gave His life when we had not yet believed. He chose us before we were born. He lavished his love without expectation. That is the love one has for their husband or wife.

Average is defined as common, typical or ordinary. When you love someone in a common way, you are not demonstrating love in a way that is different from other people.

A few years ago, I had the common practice of buying my wife a dozen roses and chocolates for Valentine's Day. I figured that if I at least showed some effort to demonstrate my love, I was doing well. So, every year, I would fight my way through the hundreds of last-minute shoppers at the local card store buying the typical card, flowers and chocolates provided. Finally, one year, my wife let out a huge sigh, and I was totally taken back at her response. "Don't you like these?" I asked. "It's fine," she responded in a cold way. That was a way to know that I was now in the proverbial dog house.

"What's wrong?" I asked, totally unaware that I had demonstrated my love in a way unacceptable. Now my heart was on my sleeve, and I couldn't see what I had done. After all, I had made an effort to buy at least something, right? Her response was branded into my mind from that day on, "These are typical gifts. These show me that you don't know me!" "I know you," I said. "Do you? Do I like chocolates?" she replied. "How can you not like chocolate, everyone likes chocolate?" I retorted. Then my wife held up the card, flowers and chocolates in a way that showed me that she meant business. "These show no thought! They are typical," she said now, fighting back tears. After wiping her tears away that seemed unstoppable, she continued, "I like gifts that show thought and consideration."

I was floored! How could I have missed something so simple? Here was my wife pulling back the curtains of revelation. It was an epiphany! From that day on, I have tried to buy gifts in a way that shows consideration. My wife is the biggest demonstrator of love in a huge way. When I make an omelet, I scramble some eggs and throw some cheese and a little meat in the middle, and "ta-da" I have something to eat. When my wife makes me an omelet, she doesn't just scramble eggs and throw cheese in and some meat. She cuts up some sweet peppers, sautés onions and chops mushrooms. She hands me a masterpiece! It's too beautiful to eat.

That is the way loving large should be. It should be practiced as a lavishing on the other person. Our love should be so overwhelming that our partner feels the effects in the soul.

Love Is More Than A Feeling

We cannot gauge love by a feeling. Love is an action. Faith does it toward the one we love, even when that person is not returning what we are investing back toward us. Feelings change with mood, and mood is impacted by our happenings and surroundings. Like the euphoria of a dance club being enamored with someone because the lights are flashing, and the beat is grooving, and we can't help but move our bodies to the beat. What happens when the mood changes or a better club opens? The feelings change for the next big thing.

God demonstrated HIS love toward us, that while we were STILL sinners, Christ died for us (see Romans 5:18). While we were yet resisting His love, He loved us. Before we ever chose to surrender our lives to Him, He loved us. That kind of love is not seen today. Often the first sign of trouble is when one or the other partner files for divorce. Today marriages are discarded like the trash we put on a curb.

The apostle Peter reminds us in 1 Peter 4:8 "Above all, love each other deeply, because love covers over a multitude of sins." The profundity of love is that it couldn't be measured by gift or value of any sort. It is beyond understanding. When you try to understand "true" love, you are trying to explore the deepness of God himself, because the Bible says God is love (1 John 4:8).

Love is so vast that it cannot be contained. It is so high that it cannot be conquered. Love is so deep that it cannot be explored. Love is so thick that its weight is far greater than gold. (See Ephesians 3:18) When we as humans attempt to define love, we are left without words. When we experience even a fraction of it, we are so overwhelmed that it is hard to contain the emotion it stirs.

Love is too large for us to hold. Yet we are called to be the embodiment of love, not just to the world, but also to those with whom we are closest. Your wife, your husband should be the recipient of a love that can only be experienced, that the overflow is something that others get the privilege of seeing and beholding.

To be large in your love, you must make room. There are areas of our life clouded by experiences too dark to decipher. Traumas in previous relationships have dictated how to be in our marriage and how to cover yourself so that you won't be damaged again. Rejection has twisted our view of the acceptance of love, so that we are constantly changing ourselves to be accepted. Like Demo Day, when a house is being remodeled or flipped, we have to tear out the plumbing of pipes that leak toxic love. Pull out walls infested with old tragic memories and dirty ideas of twisted love.

Yet we must take our time to learn to love. Loving large is not something that happens overnight. It comes by practice, and it comes by surrender to God. There is no way to love anyone unless you love them through God. Our love is shallow and superficial. God's love knows no ends.

Start by tearing out walls of unforgiveness. God knows forgiveness better than anyone. Let go of hurts that you carry with you like a pocket watch. Constantly pulling it out to remind you of wounds inflected. If God is the originator of love, we are the conduits. We allow God's love to flow through us.

Start by pulling out the times you stopped loving and forgiving yourself. If forgiving others is difficult, forgiving ourselves is stretching. It is a painful process to let go of the things you hold against yourself. Mistakes we made that hurt others. Choices we embraced that caused pain. Relationships that we should have let go, but didn't. Before you can love others, you must learn to love yourself.

The Hope I Have

I am no expert at love. I am a novice by far. Yet, I have

learned to embrace being loved by God, so that I can love my wife the only way God has loved me. I aspire to love my wife as Christ loves the church. My hope for you is that your love will grow while you read this book. I would love to think this book changed the world view of love. Even if it started with a few people.

As you read this book, do not just be a reader, apply it to every area. So many people read books and then move on to the next literary mountain. I have carefully crafted this book to help you, the reader, see love from a different perspective, God's!

A large portion of this book comes from the love chapter found in 1 Corinthians 13:1-8. As a pastor, I am aware that this book refers to the gift of love that comes from God. I am keen to see that love this chapter follows the explanation of the gifts. That being true, I know that your gifts are deemed invalid when they are not served in love.

How can you be a great husband or father when you are not serving your family in love? Your super mom efforts will be inferior when you do all that moms do for the family, if it is not done in a LARGE way.

I hope to change your mind about love for your spouse. I want to change your heart and the way you view love, and the way you live it out daily. Before you continue reading, pray this prayer:

Dear God, In Jesus' name, open my eyes to

my inconsistencies and weaknesses. Show

me where I am failing at loving my family and

my husband/wife. As I read this book, show me

how to be an example of your love. Use me

to demonstrate love to my family and friends

as well as those in need. In Jesus Name

AMEN!

LARGE LOVE IS PATIENT LOVE

The Lord is compassionate and gracious, slow to anger, abounding in love. Psalms 103:8

"Babe!" Jeff shouted from the living room, "We're going to be late!" He was waiting for his wife to finish getting ready, so they could go to an event they were invited to. Laura is usually never long in getting ready. For some unknown reason, she was running late. As he watched the hands on his watch move closer and closer to the time for them to leave, and then pass, he began to feel his patience running short. Finally, like on a big reveal, his wife came from the room looking like a cover girl model, all dolled up and looking pretty. There was only one problem, they were now late.

As the evening ran on, he just couldn't get past us being late to this event. Jeff doesn't like to run late. He tries to arrive early everywhere he goes. Both He and

Laura work hard to be on time to everything. Throughout the evening, he found himself less talkative, and shorter and abrupt in his conversations with her. Finally, she grew quiet, and the air in the car on the way home grew cold. When they arrived at home, she got out of the car and went straight into the house. It was then that he realized something was wrong.

After putting their daughter to bed, he came into the room where she had already changed her clothes and pulled back the covers. "Can we talk?" he asked. "I don't know, can we?" she responded. "You looked beautiful tonight," he said, trying to warm the atmosphere. "Did I do something wrong?" she asked. Trying to downplay his aggravation for being late, he responded, "No...I was just thinking...". "About what," she asked. "Well, I was a little bothered that we left late," he finally commented. She took what seemed like five minutes to reply, giving thought to what he had said and what she needed to say in that moment. Laura has always been that way. She is careful with her words and chooses them wisely. Where Jeff has always been abrupt in saying how he feels.

"Is that why you were so cold and quiet?" she asked. "Well, yes," he responded. Jeff continued, "I don't know why I let something so menial get under my skin, but I felt my patience wearing thin." "Do you know what I was dealing with all while I was getting myself ready?" she asked. "Um, no," he sheepishly replied. She continued, "I was getting our daughter fed, bathed, and ready all while I was trying to look nice for this event!" she said with a heated tone. Jeff had no idea and was only thinking of himself.

He felt like a jerk for allowing something like this to get under his skin. There were many things he could have done to move the night along and be more accommodating while she was getting ready. He could have avoided this whole ordeal simply by helping her and seeing her needs above his own.

Sometimes we tend to lose patience with others, and especially with those we are comfortable with. As if there is an unwritten standard, we expect others to fit a certain mold. We quickly lose our minds with people on the road. We become enraged with our children because of toys on the floor. We turn undercut and pop-shot our spouses because of some little thing that annoys us.

Patience is not only a virtue, but also a fruit. Some people are born with natural patience. My grandfather Luther was an extremely patient man. He married a woman in his youth that was promiscuous and cheated on him many times, but continued to love her. One time, she became so enraged, while drunk, that she threw a kitchen knife at him and narrowly missed him by a few inches. All the while, he stayed patient with her. He raised her children like they were his own. I suppose his chilled demeanor played a lot into his patience. I have been told by my family that I am like my grandfather.

There are few things that make me lose my temper. I often take a lot of abuse from others before I have had enough. I have had staff members who worked for me who have abused my kindness and grace. Other team members ask why I don't just fire them. I try hard to work with others to show and demonstrate Godly patience. It is when I have exhausted my patience that I finally cut things off. That is when they become shocked by my actions.

I feel that is how God is with us. The Bible says, *"The Lord is gracious and compassionate, slow to anger and rich in love."* (Psalms 145:8) He is the supreme example of how we should be toward our loved ones. The recipe for patience is very simple. Take a cup of grace and a heap of compassion. Add a dash of slow to anger and stir in a lot of love.

Grace is a key ingredient in patience. It takes grace to serve patience to others. Patience without grace is like cookies without the flour. The idea of grace or graciousness is exhibiting toward someone underserved favor or an extending of mercy where a trespass has been committed. It's closely related to forgiveness. When forgiving someone, you extend grace to them. It is knowing that a wrong has been done, yet a pass is being extended. When God is gracious, he extends mercy and favor toward us, so that we don't exhaust His patience.

In the same way, when we are patient, we are extending favor to someone who has caused us wrong or harm. We are allowing ourselves time to activate the other ingredients of this recipe for patience. Sure, that person is trying you. Yes, they are pushing all your buttons, and maybe even the ones you didn't know you had. Being gracious is like saying, without saying, I have every reason to walk away right now, but I will smile and extend my grace and mercy to you.

God is also compassionate. When you are gracious to your spouse, you want to also have compassion. For women, compassion comes much easier. They are more sympathetic toward others. Men find it much harder to be sympathetic. Compassion is the ability to have deep sympathy for another person. It is seeing them in a way that asks, "What let them be this way or do that?"

God is compassionate toward us because He sees where we have been and what we have encountered, and continues to experience that is shaping who we currently are. He knows our weaknesses, and because of his sympathy, he can extend compassion toward us. You must look at your spouse and consider them and their history that has shaped them into who they are. Have they come from an abusive home? Have they experienced a dictator type rule in their lives from a parent or former spouse?

Seeing people through God's eyes causes us to see their heart. We tend to take things personally and feel like everything our spouse does is intended to hurt us. We convince ourselves that they dream of ways to make us hurt. Although perhaps there are relationships that experience this, this isn't true for everyone. Often, we push our spouse's buttons without even knowing. Things we don't do that should have been done wear down our spouses, like the honey-do list. Things we shouldn't do that embarrass our partner, like belching in public, can drive our husband or wife insane. I know those are probably an extreme case, but you get my point.

I am having to learn how to change things about myself that I never knew were things that drive my wife nuts. In the same way, she is also evolving. We must be patient as we go through the process of evolution. We are changing from one day to the next.

Patience Is A Fruit

> *But the Holy Spirit produces this kind of fruit*
> *in our lives: love, joy, peace, **patience**, kindness,*
> *goodness, faithfulness,* Galatians 5:22 NKJV

The Bible is clear that we reap what we sow. Whatever we plant in the fertile ground of our marriage, we will get back. It is better not to sow "tares" and expect grain. Tares were a seed that looked like grain seeds, but when fully grown, they actually choked out the wheat.

The biblical proverb about the wheat and the tares shows that while something is young, they both look very similar. The only way to know the difference is when they are older, that they literally kill out the crop. In the same way, patience is a product of what we sow. We get patience when we sow grace, compassion and forgiveness.

It takes time to produce healthy and strong patience. You must understand that patience takes time to nurture. It must endure trials and testing to make it strong. When all is said and done, however, the fruit of patience will create a stronger and more enduring marriage. Marriage is hard work, and patience is a key ingredient in making it last and work. The benefits far outweigh the trials.

When you sow into your marriage, patience, you learn to love your spouse on a whole other level. You find a glimpse at what the grace of God looks like in action. We all know God's grace and have experienced His grace, but to see it in action comes when times are trying and our longsuffering wears thin.

10 so that you may live a life worthy of the Lord and please him in every way: bearing fruit in every good work, growing in the knowledge of God, 11 being strengthened with all power according to his glorious might, so that you may have great endurance and patience, Colossians 1:10-11

This verse shows us that our marriages must reflect the image of Christ and be pleasing in every way. We must sow into our marriage every good work. We must keep sowing and investing even when the return seems like it's not coming.

The process of a fruit farmer takes time. Some fruit farmers have nurtured their harvests for years. They plan their entire lives around their harvest. They know exactly when their crop will mature. They know the right times to plant seed, when to water, and when to collect the crop. Initially, the harvest seems small compared to others with a mature field. The reason for this is because your ground has not been trained.

Farmers that get a fresh property to plant and grow a harvest usually know that the first years of working the ground will not look as promising. They know that the harvest from the first years is for training the ground to give life to the fruit. As the years pass, the ground begins to yield bigger, more savory fruit. After a season, they will take a time off to let the ground rest. It's a biblical principle found in Leviticus.

When you are first married, you must know that it will take time to learn to work together. You learn each other's habits and customs. You are becoming familiar with her family and his family. You are discovering your methods for dealing with severe issues. You will face difficulties and tests of every kind, but if you keep working the ground, you will see a harvest, and the fruit of your investment will be stronger and sweeter.

Patience is also a fruit of the Spirit. If you have patience, the Holy Spirit helps us over the top. In fact, the nine fruits or characteristics of the Spirit become more evident in us the more we lean on the Holy Spirit. God sent the Holy Spirit to help us in our weakness. When we are weak in any area, such as patience, we can know that the Holy Spirit will supplement us in that area.

If you ever feel like you have no patience or that it's wearing thin, lean on the Holy Spirit, and He will help you in your time of weakness. If you your partner is pressing you and annoying you, all you can do is pray and say, "Holy Spirit, let your fruit be evident in me." God will never disappoint us when we pray and ask for His help. That is why, *"I can do all things through Christ who strengthens me."* (Philippians 4:13) When I feel I am unable to extend grace or mercy to the one I love, I know that can because it's not coming from my own personal resources, which are all but empty. It is coming from Him, whose source is endless.

When We Lose Our Patience

"Here let me do that," he said angrily as he grew impatient, not waiting for his wife to fix him a bowl of oatmeal. "No, Mark, let me do this for you," she said in reply. Grabbing the bowl of oatmeal from her hands and her letting go with equal force resulted in a shower of oatmeal all over Mark's clean shirt and tie. "Great, now look what you did! I'm going to be late for work!" he shouted. Fighting back the tears, Ashley cried, "If you had let me help you, this wouldn't have happened."

This happens almost daily in many homes and marriages today. Husbands and wives grow impatient with the process and begin to take matters into their hands. Abraham found out the consequences of growing impatient with God. God had promised Him a son and a lineage as many as the stars. In his old age, he could not see how God could possibly make this happen. He had not stopped believing, he had just grown impatient with the process.

Now Sarai, Abram's wife, had borne him no children. But she had an Egyptian slave named Hagar; [2] *so she said to Abram, "The Lord has kept me from having children. Go, sleep with my slave; perhaps I can build a family through her."* Genesis 16:1-2

Now not only was there animosity in the home between Hagar and Sarah, but also tension between Abraham's two sons. That same animosity and tension is still carried over between Isaac and Ishmael's descendants to this day.

When we grow impatient, we begin to think that we can rush the process or do things better. The result is we grow increasingly angry and embittered, and create an environment of animosity around us.

Throughout history in the Bible and man's, we see the consequences of not allowing our patience to dominate our emotional and carnal reactions.

We risk fragmenting our relationships with our spouse and others, because we become increasingly rude in our actions and attitude. Esau's impatience resulted in him selling his birthright for a bowl of lentil stew. As a result, his relationship with his brother became severed. Not to mention his brother stole his familial blessing. Impatience can cause devastation to families.

When a wife grows impatient with her husband's vices and grows weary waiting for him to change, so she starts window shopping, looking for the man that is not perfect, but better than the one she has. She travels down a dangerous road, eventually finding herself in an affair; whether emotional or sexual.

A husband who is weary of his wife's weight gain, and although she tries, she isn't fitting the fantasy he has in his mind of how she should be. So, he starts living out the euphoria of pornography. She finds out and is devastated emotionally and relationally.

Impatience costed King Saul his throne when he grew tired of waiting for the prophet to come and offer the sacrifice. He felt his over abundant sacrifice to God would bypass the disobedience that it wasn't his place. He was ordained to lead a kingdom, not offer what was only given to the priest.

Perhaps you are like Saul. When you grow weary of your husband's lack of leadership, that you take charge, because you are a getter done person. You step outside the bounds of your place in the relationship. It results in a fracture in your personal relationship with God and marital relationship with your husband.

There are many examples I could give you. The point is that when we are impatient, we are blocking God from working in us and through toward our spouse. We are a conduit of love and mercy to our loved ones. Our impatience can lead to fracturing our relationships.

We also start to create fear driven results. Don't get me wrong. Fear can be a great motivator when we use it in the right way. It can cause us to be cautious about not hurting our husband or wife. It can create awareness in us to protect and guard our family. We can also start doing things out of fear and impatience.

Because we are afraid of being let down or disappointed, we jump at something with the wrong intentions or motive. Fear is like fuel for the fire of impatience.

Another result is that we make excuses for being rude. I have been guilty of this. In the times I have been impatient, I have tried to give a reason for being rude. The truth is there is no reason for ever being rude. Kindness is like a new outfit that makes us look new, and patience is the accessory that takes you over the top.

Some people will be rude in their impatience. I was driving down the road a while back and noticed this large truck weaving in and out of traffic. When we all arrived at a red light, he kept revving his engine and taunting the car in front of him. When the light turned green, he rode on the tail of that car. Finally, when he had enough, he abruptly pulled in the lane next to him and crashed into another car. Now whatever he was in such a hurry resulted in him not arriving at all. He was driving in such a rude way that it caused others to be hurt.

I was at a well-known coffee shop and standing in line to get an order. A lady walked in dressed for success. She walked in and looked at the line and rolled her eyes. Then with a rude voice that could be heard, she said, "I need one of you to let me cut in front of you, because I am in a hurry." Not a one of us moved. After a few expletives, she commented she would never return to this coffee shop and left. When she left, the people literally cheered. Rudeness is not celebrated.

Her rude behavior resulted in not getting her the results she wanted. My wife will tell me when I grow impatient with traffic that maybe God is trying to guard us from something. She has been right about that more times than I can tell you.

There is never any reason to be rude when you have lost all patience with your husband or wife. It doesn't get results and will only drive a wedge between you and your partner.

Patience Isn't Weak, Its Focused Control

But you are merciful and gentle, Lord, slow in getting angry, full of constant loving-kindness and of truth; Psalms 86:15

I want to leave you with some thoughts on how to

focus your energy on being more patient. Because to love your spouse in a big way, your patience will have to grow.

First, patience isn't sweeping issues under the rug, it is reaching anger slowly. Another fruit of the Spirit is Self-Control. Patience and self-control are like brother and sister. They look a lot alike, but are different in many ways. Self-control, the littler sister of patience, often directs our actions, while patience controls our attitude. When things push us to lose our mind, patience says, "This is just a test, and everything will be fine." Self-control comes along in support and says, "Just calm down and think about your actions if you blow your top."

Mercy and gentleness are traits that the Father exhibits to us when we could be trying His longsuffering. They view the other person through God's eyes. God knows us better than we know ourselves. He knows what our limits are and is aware of our weaknesses. That is why he extends mercy to us; because He knows exactly when we will make them. He knows our ability to push the boundaries and cross the line of His love. He sees us and says, "Even though you deserve judgment, I still love you and will wait for you to come around. I will not force you to make choices you don't want, but I know that in the right time and season you will see what I am trying to do."

The same way God is merciful with us is the same way we must be with others. We know that man is carnal and prone to mistakes, but in the right time and season they will come around. If you have a husband or wife struggling, and you feel patience wearing thin, remember that God sees them with eyes of love.

I feel we grow impatient because we want something turned around now. We want someone to change now. We want someone to be better now. God doesn't force us to love him or come to Him, yet He can affect situations and circumstances around us that "could" drive our decisions in the right way. When we are loving large our ability to be patient, we must allow our patience to be part of the DNA markers that make up our love.

God is love (1 John 4:8) that is a fact. He is the embodiment of all that love is. Our love is weak and subject to fail and crumble. When we love large, we allow God's love and patience to shine through us.

The Fruit Of Loving Long

Imagine a perfect world where there is no suffering, pain, drama, wars, sickness, poverty, or strife. Now imagine your marriage with no problems, strife, division, or drama. Those are just a few seeds from the fruit of loving long. I say loving long, because love is not short term. First Corinthians 13:8 reminds us that "love never fails". Another way of seeing this is "Love never gives up loving." Sometimes we lose our patience and feel like we cannot possibly love someone anymore. They have worn us out, exhausted us from all possible means of understanding why they would ever hurt us or cause us pain.

Yet that is exactly how God our father loves us. He never stops loving us, even when we keep walking away from Him and put other things as a priority over Him. When we treat Him more like a lover on the side, but not as our eternal friend. He keeps loving past all our blunders.

I will admit that there are times when He remains silent and stops speaking. He may lift His hand of protection and allow the results of our sin to come in and ravage us, but it is never there because He has judged us. It is there because He cannot bear to see us continue down the path of our lives the way we do. In the same manner, you must love your spouse with the same level of love as God. He *"bears all things, hopes all things, endures all things."* (See 1 Corinthians 13:7)

Please understand that I am not saying you must stay in an abusive relationship where your life is in danger, because that is where you must show how God sometimes has to stay quiet and remove His hand for a season. What I am saying is that when you have a husband or wife that loves you and the kids, they have behaviors and attitudes that make it difficult to return that love to them. You keep showing them love by enduring those things, because you know that the seeds of your longsuffering and love will bring out a harvest.

If you are struggling with patience toward your spouse or others, make this your prayer:

CHAPTER 1 QUESTIONS FOR DISCUSSION

1. Can we discuss times in our relationship when we've had to exercise patience with each other? How did these moments make us feel?

2. How do we perceive the concept of 'patience' within the context of our relationship? Are our views aligned or do they differ?

3. Can you share a time when you had to be patient with me or when I had to be patient with you? How did that impact our relationship?

4. How can we ensure that we continue to exercise patience with each other, especially during challenging times? What practices or behaviors can we adopt to encourage this?

5. In what ways can we improve our communication to express our need for patience and understanding?

6. How can we create a safe space to discuss our challenges and practice patience with each other, even when times are tough?

7. How can we better understand and appreciate each other's needs for patience, and find ways to demonstrate it in our day-to-day interactions?

LARGE LOVE IS QUICK TO BE KIND

Be kind and compassionate to one another, forgiving each other, just as in Christ God forgave you. Ephesians 4:32

My wife is a Master of Diplomacy and tact. I have never known my wife to be rude or crass with anyone. Even in times when sitting across the table from an "enemy", she has always shown kindness and compassion. She has been known to speak her mind, but it has never been in a spirit of meanness. We have often been ridiculed for being kind to those who have not been kind to us. We have been asked why we forgive those who have wronged us. Our answer is simple, because God did that for us.

Paul wrote the to the church at Ephesus to Christians facing persecution. He was not addressing the kind of tension that comes from outside our sphere, no he was talking about that kind of strife that comes from those who are supposed to love you. He reminds his readers to walk in kindness toward one another and to have compassion and forgiveness. He wants His readers to act like children of God, not like the world.

When we face pressure from our own husband or wife, it is easy to respond with a nasty, biting comment that can easily tear down years of effort in building your marriage. One phrase from our spouse that seems or appears to be biting, and we snap back with equal tension. Paul wanted the church to follow his advice in not being like the world, not just toward our Christian friends, but our spouses as well.

Perhaps your loved one is not a Christian, what then? Peter even reminds us:

*"And now let me speak to the wives [and husbands]. Be devoted to your own husbands [spouses], so that even if some of them do not obey the Word of God, **your kind conduct may win them over without you saying a thing.**"* 1 Peter 3:1 TPT EMPHASIS ADDED

It is not through preaching at your wife or husband, but by the way you carry yourself. By the way you act toward your husband or wife, you win them to Christ. When we are constantly combative and nit-picky about everything, we are not showing kindness. I understand that picking up after a slob can be tiresome, but Peter was not referring to someone tired of picking up after their husband or wife. He was talking to women and men whose spouses were not committed to the way. As a result, they were more committed to the church and ministry of the apostles than their own husbands and wives. Instead of inspiring their loved one to become a follower, they were driving them away.

Kindness is easy to demonstrate to those who show affection toward us. When your husband or wife loves you, it will usually be instinctive to return it to them. What about showing kindness to someone is not following our way of faith? Even if they are "Christians", we tend to forget that we are demonstrators of Christ's compassion and love toward us. What if we trained and disciplined ourselves to respond quickly with kindness and compassion? Not just when our spouse is nice to us, but even when they are not. How would that change the dynamics of your marriage? How would that change you?

To walk in kindness, we must walk in humility. We must be meek in our approach toward our spouses. I say toward our spouses, because it is easier to be kinder and compassionate toward others than toward our loved ones.

I remember a time when I was snapping at my wife. I was tired and had grown familiar with her that the stresses were being spouted off on her. Yet, when I went to the church, I was more compassionate and kinder toward others. My wife pointed out that I was kinder and more watchful of my words with others than with her. She reminded me that she was my sister in sister in Christ, as well as my wife. The truth is that I had become familiar and comfortable with her, and that I took for granted what I had.

When we buy a new car, we are careful to take good care of that vehicle. We wash it regularly and clean out trash quickly. We refrain from permitting any type of eating or food in it. Over time, we begin to become so comfortable that the newness wears away. We stopped doing what we did to care for the vehicle. After a while, we start looking at other cars as potential replacements, because we miss the newness. We start to become more and more careless, never considering that if we maintain our vehicle as we did before, we will enjoy the newness every day.

Our marriages work in much the same way. If we maintain our relationships daily with care and compassion, we will enjoy it more often. I know there will be times of testing as with any marriage, but we get what we invest. The newness wears away as we lose sight of the value. Kindness comes from investing in what we have.

It's Cool To Be Kind

⁴ Even in darkness light dawns for the upright, for those who are gracious and compassionate and righteous. ⁵ Good will come to those who are generous and lend freely, who conduct their affairs with justice. Psalms 112:4-5

I was at a fast-food restaurant the other day. As I was waiting to get my order, the woman in front of me was so rude with the young lady behind the counter. I am not even sure what she was so worked up over, but she was letting this young woman experience her full wrath. Finally, the manager came and finished the order, and gave the woman extra of something just to move her along. By this time, everyone, including me, was becoming annoyed with her, and having to wait. Finally, when I came up to make my order, the girl had arrived. By this time, I started with a smile. "Well..." I started, "that was an adventure." With a nervous smile, the girl replied, "Yeah...how can I take your order?" I ordered something simple and smiled the whole time. Then I said, "I want to give 20 dollars for the person or persons behind me." She looked at me in amazement. "Really?" she asked. "Yes, I know it's not much, but maybe it will set off a reaction of some kind, right?" I spoke. I took my food and sat down in some corner of the restaurant.

The manager came over later while I was on the verge of finishing my meal and asked, "Did you give 20 dollars to pay it forward for others in line?" "Yes, I did," I said.

"That was so cool of you," he stated, "people behind you started adding to that, and only one person didn't pay for anything." I was shocked to hear that. They had 15 dollars left over by the time I had left from everyone chipping in. I would like to imagine that the gift kept giving and giving.

It is always cool to be kind. Not everyone will appreciate it. In fact, not everyone knows how to handle it. Not too many people know what kindness is.

Kindness is compassion and mercy in action. It is demonstrating love shown and received to someone else or others.

Kindness is a characteristic of love. When you love someone, you lavish them with affection. You heap on them the overflow of your love for them. Think of kindness as love in demonstration. Sometimes people will demonstrate their love by serving someone or buying a gift just because. Sometimes, kindness is exemplified by showing respect and favor. In the instance with the young lady at the restaurant, I was demonstrating a random, unexpected act of kindness to show the love of God in me.

Imagine if more people were kind? What would the world look like? Imagine if we woke each day to be kind to our partner, even if they are not kind to us. Even if they are rude and more require stiff resistance. We all want to be treated with kindness, but do we treat everyone else the way we expect or want to be treated?

So, in everything, do to others what you would have them do to you, for this sums up the Law and the Prophets. Matthew 7:12

If we want to be treated with kindness from our husbands or wives or anyone else, we must invest in them what we expect in return. Here is the catch. It may not come at first. It may come months down the road. Some investments take time to mature before they yield any type of return. Kindness starts with making your spouse breakfast in bed or doing something for them to show how great your love is. It requires daily maintenance to keep the fire lit. It depends on you not quitting and throwing in the towel on your marriage or relationship with your mate.

We make kindness cool when we can demonstrate it day in and day out. It doesn't mean you won't get tired and worn from time to time. The more you show kindness, others will see how good it is to be that way. When we do, we set the standard for kindness, and that's cool!

Nasty Is Not Nice

In the parable of the unmerciful servant (see Matthew 18:21-35), we find two people in need of kindness and mercy. Both were men in debt. One servant owed a large sum of money to a wealthy ruler, and the other owed a debt to the other servant. Most of us are all in debt to someone somewhere. By debt, I mean we need forgiveness, kindness, or mercy. You get my point.

When time came to pay the debts owed, the first servant couldn't pay. At the threat of prison, he begged for mercy (compassion and kindness) and was treated as such. When it was time for the other servant to pay, he couldn't pay his debt. However, the first servant didn't show the kindness he was afforded. Rather, he chose to be nasty about the debt. As a result, his mercy was rescinded, and he was thrown into prison.

I think that we forget the kindness that was shown to us. We become so comfortable in our forgiveness that we forget that we were in need of kindness too.

Changing Your Life Through Kindness

The Lord bless him!" Naomi said to her daughter-in-law.
"He has not stopped showing his kindness to the living
and the dead." She added, "That man is our close relative;
he is one of our guardian-redeemers." Ruth 2:20

Naomi is speaking to Ruth, her daughter in law, after Ruth explained where she had been working to glean wheat. She described Boaz, a kinsman redeemer, and a type of Christ to the church. Ruth and Naomi had moved back to Bethlehem after their tragic loss. Both widows and alone. Left without anyone to provide for them. In those days, it was not uncommon to see women who were husband-less and fending for themselves. More often than not, they were considered outcasts in society. Unless there was one in their family who would take on the responsibility of being a spouse to the women, they were destined for poverty and destitution.

These women needed kindness and understanding. They needed someone to show compassion for their need and care for their lack. Boaz was that man. The ever-perfect idea of a husband. Countless women pray for a Boaz to rescue them. In essence, what they are asking for is a husband to show kindness to them and account for their need part of their own.

Today we need spouses that demonstrate the image of Christ with such character that they exude kindness. What is all involved in showing kindness to someone? What needs to be done so that benevolence is personified not only to those in need and less fortunate, but also to our own family, starting with our spouses.

Peter was so adamant about the act of kindness that he mentions that Husbands should dwell with their wives with understanding. (1 Peter 3:7) Paul, the apostle, reminds husbands not to be harsh with their wives. Treating them as a weaker, not lessor, vessel. (Colossians 3:19) These two verses are an example of spouses responding with kindness.

My wife and I have experienced this in our own life. We have had times when we didn't like each other that much. Don't get me wrong. We loved each other, we just didn't like what the other spouse had become or had done. As a result, we have been guilty of cutting off the other by interruption. We have exemplified harshness in our words and even in our behavior toward one another. Little undercutting comments have left scars that eventually healed. It took years to learn to speak with kindness toward each other.

This isn't high school where you are dating for a season and then break up and date someone else. We were committed for life. We knew that we needed one another to survive. There are times when you will get on one another's nerves. You will drive each other crazy. You will exasperate your spouse with constant snoring, talking, weird laughs. It will seem at times that you forgot why you fell in love to begin with.

Like an aroma that fills a room, kindness when shown with genuine love can change two people. The one showing it and the one receiving it. When done with the right heart, it can change a marriage on the brink of devastation. This is the character of love. If love is large, then kindness is the legs love stands on.

Kindness is what we show everyone. When you are kind to others, it is because you have reasoned inside of yourself that you would rather be kind than be right. Sometimes we forget that the person we fight and hurt with our words and actions is the person who loves us the most. There is never a reason to be rude.

Being rude is like a cold glass in hot water. It seasons the ground for a lot of trouble and retaliation. What would have happened had Boaz not shown kindness to Ruth? What if he had said to her, "Get out of here, you beggar!" Yet, he didn't do that. He gave her what others felt she didn't deserve. He covered when she was exposed. He fed her and gave her an overflow. In return, she covered his feet a sign of surrender and submission.

We treat our friends and their wives better than we treat our wives. We treat our husband's friends better than our husbands. We talk back, shoot verbal jabs below the belt when we are irritated. All these are rude. Imagine if Christ fed an emotional comment below the belt when you come to Him with a need?

"Dear Jesus," we pray, "Help me to get this job promotion." Jesus responds, "Why, so you can screw this up like the last one?" Instead, Jesus patiently and lovingly takes us through times of testing and preparation to set us on a right path for what we have asked.

We must remember that kindness reflects the Love of God within us. When we are rude, we are saying, that God's love is not in us.

CHAPTER 2 QUESTIONS FOR DISCUSSION

1. In your perspective, what does kindness mean specifically within the framework of our relationship? How does this understanding align or differ with mine?

2. Could you recount a particular moment when I showed kindness to you? How did this act make you feel and how did it influence your perspective towards our relationship?

3. What are your thoughts on how consistent acts of kindness can shape our relationship? Can we discuss the long-term impacts of kindness on our bond?

4. Let's reflect on a situation where it was difficult for us to show kindness to each other. How did we navigate this challenge and what could we have done differently to foster kindness instead?

5. How do you think you can enhance the way you express kindness towards me? Are there specific actions or behaviors you'd like to work on?

6. How can we better support each other in our endeavor to practice more kindness in our relationship? Are there any specific strategies or methods we can adopt?

7. What are some practical steps we can integrate into our daily routine as a couple to foster more acts of kindness?

LARGE LOVE DOES NOT ALLOW ENVY

Let us not become conceited, provoking, and envying each other. Galatians 5:26

My wife is a gifted singer. Her voice can send chills up your spine and make your heart skip a beat. When she sings people are amazed that all that voice can come out of her small five-foot frame. I, on the other hand can sing, but am not a gifted singer, in my opinion. When we were first married, we sang as a duet quite often. Yes, our voices complimented each other as we would sing and perform our songs at various events.

My wife would often get asked to sing solo at many events. In the beginning years of our marriage, I saw us as a duet but began to feel envious that she would get asked to sing solos more than me. Today, I know that I am not the sing that she is, but in those days, I felt that I was had more experience and knowledge of music theory. My envy began to put a strain on our marriage to the point that my wife held back her singing. She turned down opportunities because she didn't want me to feel jealous of what doors were opening for her.

"I feel like you held me back," she cried one night as we got into one of our heated arguments. I tried to debate my case and say, "I thought we were a couple and were going to build our ministry of singing together." My immature nature could not understand what singing meant to her. I became mean and conceited that when I felt she was too pitchy. When I would snap at her for various reasons, all related to my stupid envy, I would drive her to simply shut down.

In our foundational verse love is not only selfless, it refuses to be jealous when blessings come to someone else. The definition of jealousy means to be intolerant of rivalry or unfaithfulness. Vigilant in guarding a possession. Envy, however, refers to painful or resentful awareness of an advantage enjoyed by another joined with a desire to possess the same advantage.

Jealous love says, I refuse to compete for your affection with someone else or anything else. Imagine you love a certain hobby so that it takes all your time and focus. You invest in it. You talk about it to the point that your spouse is left out of connection with you. In fact, your partner must compete with your hobby for affection. So, your husband or wife says, "It's me or your hobby!" That is what jealous love is! That is why God is jealous for us. He wants our affection and attention. When we are turning our hearts and attention to other things he will not compete for our affection. We must know all that He has done for us so that we will turn our love to Him out of love.

Envious love says, "I am bothered that you got something that I didn't, and I want it too." When you love someone, you are proud of their accomplishments and happy to see them succeed. You celebrate their achievements with them! When you are envious of your spouse you make it hard for yourself to love them. They love you and will give up something for you, but it is impossible to love someone and still be envious of them at the same time.

Why Does Envy Destroy Marriages?

Envy is a powerful weapon that the enemy uses to destroy marriages. He works overtime with spouses who become covetous toward what the other spouse has. Lucifer before he was cast out of heaven because envious of God. The worship that used to go through him he wanted for himself. Perhaps he saw how worship moved God's presence, but he allowed himself to become so resentful that he said:

13 For you said to yourself, 'I will ascend to heaven and set my throne above God's stars. I will preside on the mountain of the gods far away in the north. 14 I will climb to the highest heavens and be like the Most High.' Isaiah 14:13-14 NLT

The very one that he worshiped he longed to become. He envied the Most High God and wanted to become like God. Satan knows how to work envy into your relationships so that you cause your own destruction.

It is interesting to know how the enemy begins working in the root of resentment into your marriage so that it destroys not just the couple but the entire family. He masterfully weaves his plan from the beginning of that person's life until they are met with one devastating blow after another.

Take a young boy who strives to meet his father or mother's approval. He tries and tries and never seems to meet their standard. Yet, he sees his sibling who strives less and does less get more attention, affection, and acceptance that he does. As he goes about life, he experiences these same traumatic experiences in almost every situation. At work he works hard to be on time, stay late, do more than his share only to be passed up by someone who is the complete opposite. His heart is like a millstone around his neck, slowly pulling him deeper and deeper into a psychotic blindness.

In his marriage he works hard to show love and affection to his wife. He helps around the house. He does all he can to express his love to his wife. The first sign of criticism he meets from his spouse sounds like a rejection. She thinks she is helping him; he thinks she is discrediting his affection and love. She comes home with news of a promotion at work, and he feels like he is going to blow a gasket. "Why is she getting promoted? I work harder than she does, and she gets promoted? She's a woman."

Like that he is on a downward spiral. He becomes moody and emotional. She is left confused and trying to figure out what is going on. He even feels rejected and competing with the kids for her affection. And, because she is confused and feeling emotional abused by his tirades she withdraws from his romantic advances.

All the while the devil is left laughing at the portrait of devastation he has painted. He celebrates every line and detail he crafted with his lies and deception.

What Does Envy Cause?

Envy leads to resentment in your spouse because they want you to be happy with them. They want you to celebrate their wins. They want you to be happy for their achievements. They want to know you are in their corner cheering them on but when you are covetous and resentful of their achievements or happiness you are slowly suffocating their joy. Resentment is when you are displeased or indignant at someone's remark or actions. Resentment says I am envious of your achievements because I cannot or have not been able to reach that level. Really, resentment becomes a reflection of fear. Fear that our partner will achieve some level of success and think little of us because we haven't accomplished what they have. Fear that if they get promoted that they will become way too busy to be with us. Dread that they will find someone to replace us. It's these responses that create unhealthy and unspiritual behavior that we act out on.

We begin to demonstrate resentment through our words. Small little, tiny words that work like a thousand little daggers slowly cutting at the fiber of your partners emotions, mind frame and heart. Those emotions begin to feed on the drama that we are concocting in our minds and the little words begin to turn into a monster of emotions that begins to dominate and contaminate our actions.

As we give in to our inner hulk, that green monster of rage and resentment that only comes out when provoked, we start creating catastrophic damage. Our partners begin to pull away as our beast of bitterness clears a path for us to walk on.

There is no room for envy in marriage. Love is not envious. It is not competitive with our spouses. It is happy for our partner. It is excited that they win becomes their win is our win. Their achievements reflect on us and not solely on them. Envy is not the same as jealousy.

The definition of jealousy is that we are intolerant of rivalry or unfaithfulness. Envy is defined as painful or resentful awareness of an advantage enjoyed by another joined with a desire to possess the same advantage.

In other words, when your spouse works a lot and seldom spends time with you and the kids, you become jealous of your partner's job. When your spouse spends time with their friends and is rarely home because they are always there, you can be jealous of your husband or wife's unfaithfulness to the marriage. Envy is different in that it wants what the other has and becomes combative or belligerent because of what they have.

It is impossible to love someone and still be envious of them at the same time. When you love someone, you celebrate them and their accomplishments. You are cheering them on whether they win or lose.

Envy In Marriage Causes Resistence

Once your spouse feels the tension of envy, they become resistant to you and your advances. They are leery of your compliments. They are weary of your feeble attempts at humility. They become closed off and begin to stone wall your advances and attempts at being romantic.

Take for example Josh and Nina. They had been married for seven years. During this time both, he and his wife, work in the real estate industry. Josh approaches his work with a certain lackadaisicalness. He waits to promote homes. Seldom carries his business cards with him. He can sell and in the past was good at marketing. Yet, because of his lukewarm approach he is frustrated that he is not more successful.

Nina is successful. In fact, she seems to be born for this industry. Several times she has been on the top sellers list. She closes more than ten homes in one month compared to Josh's two or three. She loves what she does and excels at it effortlessly. But tension is starting to build between the two. Nina knows that her wins are Josh's wins and vice versa, yet that is not how he sees it. He is beginning to envy Nina's successes. He wants what she has.

Not only has Nina been on the top sellers list, but she has also been recognized by the state and national realtors' association as up-and-coming stars to watch for. She has been recognized for her contributions to society and planning of entire communities. Josh has not even come close. Up until now, Josh had been content to sell enough houses to get by.

In a fit of resentment, he spits out pot shots like his mouth is an AK-47. He undercuts her achievements as minuet. When at the breaking point he blurts out like hot lava that she must have slept her way to where she is and insinuates that she has been unfaithful. Nina runs out tearful and wounded by Josh's words. How could someone she loves to be so mean and hurtful? How could he not be happy for her successes?

When Josh closed his first three homes, she made a special dinner and celebrated his wins! In the beginning he celebrated her as well, but as her wins began to overshadow his he began to feel envy eating away at him. He tried hard to not let what he was feeling overwhelmed him, but the more she achieved the more he grew more bitter. She couldn't help that she was good at what she did.

Initially, they made up and skirted their blow up. She decided that she didn't want to make him upset and didn't want him to feel less successful, so she paused her workload and decided to focus on being a wife. Yet, he still held on to resentment and envy.

Finally, his attempts at being romantic were tabled with comments like, "I'm feeling tired," or, "I need to clean the kitchen," or some other excuse. She began to put up walls of resistance. His envy, like a battering ram, has destroyed the foundation of their once solid relationship.

There are so many Joshes and Nina's out there. It's not just men envying their wives. Sometimes it is wives envying their husbands. In either case that envy if not addressed and surrendered will tear away from the fabric of that marriage.

Envy In Marriage Causes Rebellion

Envy can lead to all sorts of rebellious and selfish behavior in your marriage relationship. The idea that if our spouse is not happy for us then we need to be happy alone. God has ordained for there to be order in our lives because He is a God of order.

Marcus and Ronda were a happy couple, or so they thought. They did everything together. They sang together in the choir at church, and she often sang with the frontline singers. Marcus became envious of her always being asked to sing up front. "Why do you always get asked to sing and not me?" he asked her emotionally. "I don't know Marcus, I will ask them to consider you to sing up front too," she responded. "I don't want them to do it because you asked them to, I want them to see that I can sing as good as you," he spat back.

Things seemed to have calm down as Ronda was not asked to sing for several weeks then suddenly, she was asked to sing again and not him. In a fit if resentment Marcus leaves and goes out with some friends and begins to drink to the point of getting drunk. Something he had never done before. He stops going to church with her, anything that involves singing with Ronda he shuts down. They used to sing together in the car, but now he puts an end to it before it even starts.

Rebellion is as the sin of witchcraft the bible says, that means that rebellion brings along with it the character and nature of those who do evil. Marcus was not being rebellious toward Ronda, but toward God because Ronda was being shown the favor, he felt that he deserved.

How Do We Bounce Back From Envy?

First envy is a sin in the eyes of God, because God does not envy. When you read 1 Corinthians 14:4-8 we are learning that this is the nature of God. When we have God Spirit in our lives we are responding to others, not just our spouses with the same character and nature of God. So, God is not envious. He celebrates our wins with us. When we become envious it is because we are not allowing His nature to flow through us and giving place to the devil for him to establish residency.

Second, we must be willing to recognize envy at its core. We must be aware of its side effects and characteristics so that we can recognize when we are becoming envious of someone we love. Ask yourself, "Why am I envious of someone I love and their accomplishments?" Just because I don't have the same achievements does not mean that I cannot be genuinely happy for them and with them.

Third, ENVY is a mental stronghold that we must be willing to surrender to God. After we have recognized it in our lives, we must be willing to repent of envious behavior and put on the mind of Christ (Philippians 2:5). This is not a one-time deal. Putting on the mind of Christ involves studying the attitude, character, and behavior of Christ over and over and comparing ourselves to Him. It requires constant review of small seemingly insignificant areas and repenting of them before they take root. Envy has no place in the life of a Christian. It has no place in a marriage if it is going to work peacefully and with God's blessing.

Lastly, we must allow ourselves to be vulnerable and receive correction and instruction; even if it is from our spouse, a pastor or mentor. Vulnerability means that we become transparent about our struggle with envy and be willing to receive guidance while we find our way to true celebration and happiness for our spouse. As long as we take on these areas, we will find peace and happiness in love.

Chapter 3 Discussion Questions

1. Have there been times when envy has affected our relationship? If so, can we discuss those instances and how they made us feel?

2. How do you perceive envy? Do you see it as a natural human emotion, a destructive force, or something else?

3. Can you share a time when you felt envious of something in my life? How did you handle that feeling and what can we do to better address such feelings in the future?

4. How can we support each other when one of us is feeling envious, whether it's envy towards each other or towards others?

5. How can we ensure that envy does not negatively impact our appreciation for what we have in our relationship?

6. In what ways can we turn feelings of envy into positive actions or conversations that can strengthen our relationship?

7. How can open communication help us manage feelings of envy? Can we establish some guidelines or strategies for discussing this emotion when it arises?

LARGE LOVE DOES NOT BRAG

Love does not brag about one's achievements nor inflate its own importance. 1 Corinthians 13:4b TPT

I have learned over the years that bragging was simply an overcompensation for the feeling of insignificance and self-worth. Early on in our marriage to my wife, Rose, I found myself bragging about things I had done in my life. All too many times I would exaggerate about my small achievements to make myself look better. Call it posturing. I could not see at the time how God had brought me before great people. My self-worth was so low that I felt I needed to boast about my own abilities rather than rest in my identity and gifts.

This began to trickle into my marriage. Because I would be envious of my wife and the favor God showed upon her life, I felt I needed to brag about my own achievements and exaggerate my own importance. I knew that my wife was a woman of great strength, talent, and ability, yet rather than allow her to compliment me gifts, I felt the need to compete. Hence, the reason why I would envy her.

When I read this verse, it is conveying the message that boasting is a vein display of one's own achievements or worth. It's a position of posturing to make oneself look better than or greater than the other person. You would have to feel insignificant to build yourself up over your spouse. In the place where we should feel free to be ourselves.

We've all been in that situation. You've been cornered by someone who boasts about his or her wonderful life, intelligence, and achievements. You may be able to gracefully escape at times, but you may be stranded at others.

According to Merriam-Webster, the word brag means "to talk boastfully; to demonstrate haughty and pompous discourse."

When you think of someone who is "a class act," you probably think of someone who is gracious, humble, and confident while remaining inconspicuous. Someone who does not brag about themselves.

So, what exactly is going on here? My investigation

yielded several theories, all of which revolved around the same central theme. People boast because they are self-conscious. They want to be accepted, but they aren't sure how. As a result, it's as if their mouth is telling their brain that they are truly good enough.

Braggers put forth a lot of effort — weaving intricate stories — to gain the admiration, they desire. They're typically motivated by a deep fear or fury that they don't measure up, and as a result, they overcompensate.

One's life experiences contribute to this insecurity. People can develop this phobia as early as childhood, with a fear of abandonment, or if their parents instilled conditional rather than unconditional love in them. Individuals who brag often are unaware that they are doing so. Even yet, those vexing conversations can be difficult to bear.

One example of when someone one-ups someone else reminds me of Jack and Ben. They were known for their friendly rivalry, but Ben had a peculiar habit of always trying to "one-up" Jack.

One sunny afternoon, they sat in the local café, sipping their coffees. Jack, an avid birdwatcher, started the conversation, "You know, Ben, I spotted a rare blue jay in my backyard yesterday."

Ben, not missing a beat, responded, "That's interesting, Jack. But just last week, I saw a pair of golden eagles nesting in the tree next to my house."

Jack, slightly taken aback, continued, "That's impressive, Ben. Speaking of nature, I've started a small vegetable garden. I even harvested some fresh tomatoes this morning."

Ben, with a smirk, replied, "That's wonderful, Jack. However, I've been running a full-fledged organic farm in my backyard for a year now. I even supply my produce to the local market."

Jack, determined not to let Ben's one-upmanship get to him, said, "I've taken up painting recently. It's a great stress-reliever."

Ben quickly retorted, "Painting, you say? I've had my artwork displayed at the local gallery. In fact, one of my pieces was sold last month."

Jack sighed and smiled, realizing that no matter what he said, Ben would always find a way to one-up him. However, he didn't let it bother him. He knew his achievements were significant in their own right, and he didn't need to compare them with anyone else's. And so, the friends continued their conversation, with Jack sharing and Ben one-upping, just another typical day in the small town of Oakville.

Bragging Is Not Godly Character

For the world offers only a craving for physical pleasure, a craving for everything we see, and pride in our achievements and possessions. These are not from the father but are from this world. 1 John 2:16 NLT

A marriage cannot be healthy if one spouse is always outdoing the other. Everything cannot be enjoyed if the atmosphere for sharing is not there. In 1 John 2:16 the apostle John starts with a warning. What is that warning? *"For the world offers only a craving for physical pleasure, a craving for everything we see, and pride in our achievements and possessions."*

Having the need to be affirmed for our appearance, accomplishments, or possessions is the source of bragging. Most often, people who brag do so because they feel small and want to be acknowledged and made to feel as significant as they see themselves. The act of bragging in marriage often elevates one spouse over the other, so much so that one feels like they aren't up to the standard the other has set for themselves.

A form of bragging, which is a form of self-promotion and self-glorification, naturally tends to be unhealthy.

There are times when boasting can cause more friction and turmoil than needed in a Christian marriage, where humility is an essential requirement.

Sometimes, when one is bragging, the act of egotism to make oneself seem important is as foolish as the person who is doing the boasting. In reality, there is something deeper going on that the partner cannot see or didn't see before the marriage. As a result, bragging, causes our partners to feel less than and will create pressure that can eventually provoke a retaliation.

Jenny had always struggled with low-self-esteem and as a result she would overcompensate by bragging about her accomplishments, no matter how insignificant they were. She felt that her achievements would help her to feel more important. She would often brag about people she met or saw even if it were from afar. Whenever anyone would challenge her or question what she was saying she would exhibit what counselors call, "Ape-Mentality."

The Ape Mentality is often acted out by someone who, when feeling threatened, tries to establish territory. Much like an Ape that pounds their chest or the ground to establish territory she would ramp up her chest pounding by using phrases such as, "Well, I even did this and if that's not believable I also met or did…". As a result, people that once called her a friend found themselves cutting her off. Her boasting became exhausting and draining.

How Does One Deal With A Spouse That Brags?

When dealing with a bragging partner it is essential to not make them feel cornered. When cornered they will often come out fighting and retaliating. They will sooner cut you off before you can cut them.

When confronting a bragging spouse timing is crucial in helping them to see how their habitual boasting is affecting their community that surrounds them. Bad behavior is never okay. We are all guilty of bragging in some form. It's part of our human nature. Yet, when bragging puts us above our loved one it becomes wrong and requires adjusting.

Start by asking, "Hey, can we talk? I heard you say something that I want to provide some feedback about." This will help to open the conversation and initiate dialog.

Your conversation could sound something like this.

You: Hey, can we talk? I heard you say something earlier that I want to provide some feedback."

Them: Okay? What did I say?

You: You mentioned that you met (famous person) last month when we went out, I was with you that night. Why don't I remember meeting them?

Them: Oh, I ran into them in the restroom in the restaurant. It's no big deal.

You: I don't want to create something here, but tonight was the first time I heard about this. I just wanted to talk about this with you because it seemed like you were bragging.

Them: Bragging? I wasn't bragging.

You: Like I said, I'm not wanting to start something, I just noticed that when Tom and Hillary mentioned that they went to Hollywood they met (famous person) and then you chimed in that you met (famous person) who seems to be more famous than (famous person).

Them: And your point is?

You: It just seemed like you had to one up them. It is totally fine if you met (famous person) in the restroom or even on the street, but it was Tom and Hillary's party and it may not have been the time to outdo them.

Them: I wasn't trying to outdo them. It came to my mind

that I had met someone famous too, but now that I think about it, I can see how it could have sounded.

From there the conversation can be carried in a healthy way and become more productive.

So What Does The Bible Say About Bragging

For the world offers only a craving for physical pleasure, a craving for everything we see, and pride in our achievements and possessions. These are not from the Father but are from this world. 1 John 2:16 NLT

We can often be tempted in many ways. In marriage we can feel as if we are insignificant and left out when our spouse is being appreciated, when we should be celebrating them for their achievements. These only make for a toxic relationship and environment. It is never wrong to achieve and succeed. It is never wrong to give one hundred percent in your job, it is okay when you do so to take pride in your work. Even God looked over all he created and saw that it was good. Boasting however takes us and places us above others so that we feel important and so that others view us as important.

If you are aware that you are boasting the best thing to do is become aware and stop. If you have some so in a way that has made your spouse, feel less than acknowledge your behavior and ask for forgiveness. Moving forward you will feel the urge at times to speak out when you feel unimportant. Here is a great way to remind yourself.

Remember that you are important to your spouse in that very moment. Their success is also yours and bragging on yourself only belittles their success in whatever and causes you to become a blackhole and not a guiding light. In times when they succeed, celebrate them. Ask them how their accomplishment makes them feel. Tell them you are proud of them and cannot wait to see what they do next.

As you make a practice of this you will find it easier to celebrate wins and much more difficult to brag on yourself.

CHAPTER 4 DISCUSSION QUESTIONS

1. Can we discuss any instances when either of us felt the other was bragging or boasting? How did that make us feel?

2. How does it affect our relationship when one of us brags about personal achievements? Does it create competition or friction?

3. What do you think motivates us to brag or boast? Is it a need for validation, a desire to impress, or something else?

4. How can we communicate our accomplishments or good news to each other without it coming across as bragging?

5. How do you feel when I share my achievements with you? Is there a way I can do it that would feel more supportive and less like boasting?

6. In what ways can we express pride in each other's accomplishments without it coming across as bragging?

7. How can we create an environment where we both feel valued and appreciated for our accomplishments, without the need to brag or boast?

LARGE LOVE DOES NOT TRAFFIC IN SHAME

"Love does not traffic in shame and disrespect, nor selfishly seek its own honor..." I Corinthians 13:5a TPT

Jenny was raised in church and never thought she would have ever cheated on her husband. Her mom and dad had been married for over 40 years and demonstrated a wholesome marriage to her and her siblings. She never would have imagined that she would have ever done something that others find unmentionable. Yet, it happened.

When it all came out, she was mortified. Her husband, Chase, was crushed beneath a load of anger, resentment, embarrassment, and feelings of insufficiency. The thoughts in his head were often coming at him a thousand miles an hour. Not just one thought, but it seemed like thousands. He often felt himself sleepless at night. Questions kept passing through his mind. "Why, would she do that?" "Am I not good enough for her?" "What did she see in him that she didn't see in me?"

Then, questions turned to anger and denial. "How could she be so selfish?" "How dare she violate our vows?" "If I ever saw that guy I would..." While Jenny's husband was dealing with the emotional and mental devastation; Jenny was left still caring for the kids and working a full-time job. While Chase buried himself in work to avoid being home, Jenny would work and then come home to an empty house with just her and the kids. She would occupy herself with helping the kids with their schoolwork and projects. She would feed them and then put them to bed. When Chase came home the air grew tense. He would often fall asleep with his back to her. The only time they talked was if it was about the children.

"When are we going to talk, Chase?" she asked. "I have nothing to say," he responded. "I'm lonely," I can't do this on my own," she would say. "Why, don't you call your boyfriend," since you seemed to be so fond of him," Chase would fire back. Tension would build as both dealt with emotional pain.

On Chase's social media page, he would put quotes about people who cheat, and Jenny would feel even more devastated. At church they would walk in, and people would just stare at her and talk quietly under their breath as she walked by. She just knew that he had created speculation in their minds.

Finally, Chase agreed to go to counseling. He was willing to talk to someone. At first his expectations were low. He had his heart set on divorcing Jenny. He couldn't bear the thought of being with someone who could even consider cheating. His heart was so blocked with walls of distrust that for the first few weeks he scarcely said two words. When the counselor asked him questions, he responded in as few words as possible.

"Look, you need to ask yourself. Do I love my wife?" The counselor asked Chase. For what seemed like an eternity he sat in silence. The longer he took to respond the more Jenny felt the stream of tears flowing down her face. Then, out of the darkness a glimmer came through as he responded. "Yes," he answered in a choking voice. It was easy to see the word was stuck under the Adams apple in his throat. He was struggling to let the words come out. Everything within him struggled to find the words. It was as if his anger was holding on to every word like a vice.

"I love her, but I feel so betrayed," he said as one tear turned to two and three. He began to weep, "I never thought the person I loved so much would betray me so deep." I love her and want to trust her, but my gut is telling me not to," he continued. Without saying a word, he reached over and took Jenny by the hand and like flood gates she began to sob.

"I am sorry that I did what I did," she said in between weeping breaths. "I'm sorry I betrayed your trust in me," she continued. With tears pouring like a waterfall down his rugged face, he turned and said, "I forgive you."

Then he continued, "I'm sorry for uncovering you and bringing you shame." She pulled away with a look of confusion. "What do you mean?" she asked. "I had confided in Nick at church and Nick told his wife. Now everyone knows. I am not sure how to get that back," Chase confessed.

The counselor sat smiling and almost as teared up as the couple sitting before him. "Shame and guilt are what we find ourselves doing when others have wronged us," he said. "You don't have to walk in shame anymore," he continued. "Chase, the way to offset that shame is by apologizing to others about what you said concerning your wife," said the counselor. "Jenny, you don't have to walk in shame because you know that your husband has forgiven you, and that all things are made new," he continued.

The next Sunday, Chase and Jenny walked into church

with their kids in tow and the biggest smiles on their faces. She held Chase's hand and a gesture of safety, and he walked in with his hand in hers and a look of protection over her.

Cases like this happen all the time. Not just in church, but even in everyday scenarios. When we feel betrayed, we often allow our emotions to dictate our actions. As a result, we create shame and embarrassment for the ones we love, that have most likely have hurt us.

What Causes Us To Shame Others

While we focus in on the first part of our opening verse, I want to direct your attention to what the passage says:

Love does not traffic in shame and disrespect...

For us to traffic in shame it means that we are directing others to look at our loved on or someone else in a shameful way. Take for example the sinful woman that was about to be stoned by the pharisees. Although, they didn't love her, they were to be an example of God's love toward others. Rather they became leading traffickers into her shame.

The anatomy of shame often starts with exposing someone to others. By exposing them we are revealing their actions, attitudes, and behaviors to cause them embarrassment. Then our actions provoke others to create judgment toward our loved on. Often, we feed others information that may not be complete or may be our own opinion of the situation. Anytime you are manipulating others' opinions of someone else you are trafficking in shame.

To traffic shame means that you are directing others' opinions, and judgments to create a system or atmosphere of manipulation or control. With that control we can begin to manipulate someone we "loved" into doing what we want or else. This is not love.

We want to control things that we don't feel secure about. That is why parents will manipulate children with fear. That is why spouses will manipulate a partner using tactics such as abuse (verbal, emotional, mental, and physical) as a means of getting their way. Trafficking in shame is an abusive action that seeks to control a situation. When control is being used as a weapon of destruction it creates tension.

Manipulation is a selfish attitude and action. We treat people like puppets to control them. The problem is there is no honor in controlling others. God, who is sovereign and all-powerful created mankind and never seeks to control his creation. He allows us to choose. We can choose to serve Him and experience freedom from sin and have eternal life, or we cannot serve Him and our freedom is shallow and short lived. It becomes based on our emotional and mental happiness.

God Honors Us When We Honor Others

Honoring others is viewed by God as number one on the list of character traits we all should have. Why? Because God loves honor. If honor were not important to God, He would not have mentioned it one hundred and forty-seven times throughout the bible. When shame is trafficked in it takes away from that honor. In fact, exposing others sin and shaming them is dishonoring. God cannot work in the confines of our desire to dishonor.

The word dishonor is defined as a lack or loss of honor or reputation. Trafficking in shame or revealing another person's shame is causing them to become dishonored. I know, you are probably thinking, "Wait, so am I supposed to cover another's persons sin?" The answer is no. We are to expose the deeds of darkness, yet we there is a recipe for how we are to approach someone else while maintaining honor.

The bible is clear that we are to approach others in the Spirit of Gentleness and Love. It is only when they remain unrepentant are we to expose them. The bible never gives us a green light to shame someone publicly. Think about how you would feel if God exposed your deeds before those you love. How shameful would you feel? Yet, God doesn't do that. He loves us and brings personal and private conviction so that change is made. Its only when we remain unrepentant that He allows our sin to be exposed and that is often by our own doing and not His.

Through love you confront and through love you wait patiently for others to come around. This is honoring others.

You can dishonor your spouse by complaining to your friends or family about them without them present. This is dishonoring. God cannot honor you when you dishonor others. We want others to feel compassion for our pain. We want attention for grief, and we want those who have hurt us to feel the pain we feel. Yet, this is not only unhealthy, but also destructive and cause problems and even divorce or separation in your relationship.

Majority of marriage problems would be resolved if we would stop dishonoring our spouses. How do we dishonor them? We dishonor our spouses by whole plethora of ways, but none are as devastating as trafficking in shame. It would be as if we took our spouse and paraded them in front of others making them wear a scarlet letter or a sign exposing their wrong. The way to win your spouse is through loving them even when they are not capable of loving themselves.

To honor someone is to value them highly or bestow value upon them. Which is more valuable? An artifact that has no damage and yet has no story or an artifact that has history and shows signs of wear and maybe even damage.

Let's reflect at Jenny. She cheated on Chase, her husband. His responses toward her could have been so different. Sure, he was injured by her actions. Yes, he felt betrayed, but what if he had embraced her and hey would have had a mature conversation. In love he could have stated his feelings and his pain, and she would have felt the weight of her actions. Yet, he also could have expressed his love toward her and helped her to realized that they were going to make it through. He could have expressed his disappointment in her decision and that his trust is set back, but at the same time could have expressed to her his love for her and that he forgives her how he would want to be forgiven.

Imagine the freedom she would have felt. She would have been able to walk in healing and the two, together would have walked in healing as they rebuild this area of their lives. Sure, it's hard, to get past feelings betrayal or hurt and pain. Everything in us wants to run and start over again. Every thought screams out, who knows and what are they thinking. Honor helps us restore what was lost, stolen or damaged and exemplifies the amazing grace of God.

Two Ways To Honor Your Spouse

Do nothing from selfishness or empty conceit, but with humility of mind regard one another as more important than yourselves; Philippians 2:3 (NASB)

When we love large, we are working past the selfness and empty conceit to see others as more important. We are putting to practice the principle to loving your neighbor as yourself. When you love someone, you are careful how you treat them. My wife often reminds me that she is God's priceless treasure of which I am a steward.

How I steward my spouse is essential in how God honors me. If I am not faithful in the lessor things God cannot honor me with greater things. Not that my spouse is insignificant. She is God's best for me. If I cannot demonstrate that she is God's blessing in my life, how can I expect God to bless me in other areas of my life.

So, I have added two ways that you can honor your spouse. Read them and practice them and see if they will not change your life.

1) Watch how you speak to them.

What we say is as important and how we say it. I know sometimes we feel that if we don't say things in harsh way things will never get done or things will never change.

Let your conversation be gracious and attractive so that you will have the right response for everyone. Colossians 4:6

The way to honor your spouse is not only in how you treat them, but in how you speak to them. Harsh words stir up resentment and provoke an unwanted response.

A gentle answer deflects anger, but harsh words make tempers flare. Proverbs 15:1

We must become good at choosing our words. We must practice the art of saying things that edify and build up. When we use our words to tear down, we are only destroying our lives and our children's lives as well.

2) For every criticism you say offer three positive things that they do.

It is easy to criticize other. I know, I've done it. When we dislike something, we can say things that are destructive. There was a time when I was very destructive with my words. I used my words to manipulate and control.

It is easy to tell someone what we hate about them, but what about what we do like about them. "You know what your problem is? You are too easily controlled." Okay? So, since you saw that in me how do I fix it. Any suggestions?

When we are in the heat of an argument, we will often spew out words, like a volcanic eruption, carelessly wiping out any semblance of hope in our spouse. We will spit venomous phrases that seek to gain advantage rather than seek to heal.

Don't use foul or abusive language. Let everything you say be good and helpful, so that your words will be an encouragement to those who hear them. Ephesians 4:29

In our rage filled rants we can often use foul or course language. I know, most often we don't try to use it to control, knowingly. Instead, we use it to gain advantage in the moment.

Have you ever said something in the heat of an argument and then later said, "I didn't mean it." These words often tear down and destroy. Coarse language sets the other person off their course of thinking and usually results in both parties fighting for ground.

In marriage, we must take care to remember than often children are involved and are hearing every word we say. Our words become the next generations textbooks and our actions become their education.

In arguments, rather than traffic in shame, remembering and bringing up a laundry list of shameful works. Instead, For every one critique bring up three qualities that you love or for everyone judging comment, offer three suggestions for changing that behavior or action.

If you are a Christian reading this book. Let me remind you that others will know that we are Christians by our love for one another. Not just our friends at church, but our spouses as well.

CHAPTER FIVE DISCUSSION QUESTIONS

1. Can we discuss any instances where either of us felt shamed or disrespected in our relationship? How did those experiences make us feel?

2. How do we define respect within the context of our relationship? How does this definition align or differ for both of us?

3. How do you feel when your actions or words are criticized in a way that makes you feel ashamed or disrespected? How can we address these feelings?

4. Can we discuss the impact of shame or disrespect on our relationship? How does it affect our communication, trust, and overall relationship dynamic?

5. What steps can we take individually and together to ensure that we communicate and behave in ways that foster respect and avoid shaming?

6. How can we create a safe space to talk about instances where we've felt shamed or disrespected, and work towards healing and understanding?

7. How can we better understand each other's sensitivities to avoid unintentionally triggering feelings of shame or disrespect?

LARGE LOVE DEFENDS AGAINST OFFSENSES

Love is not easily irritated or quick to take offense. 1 Corinthians 13:5 b TPT

Does your spouse get on your nerves? Does it seem like they know the right buttons to push so that you lose control? Often when we have been married for a long time or in a relationship for quite some time, we can get comfortable to allow certain bad habits go. We can also get annoyed by our spouse's little quirks that never seem to go away. These little annoyances seem insignificant but can eventually add up later.

Phillip and Maria have been married for twelve years. When they first fell in love, they couldn't get enough of each other. Phillip would make Maria laugh with his corny jokes and his comical antics. She would laugh so hard that her sides hurt from all the laughter.

Phillip practically fell head over heels for Maria the first time he saw her. She was dressed so perfectly. She took time to care for her appearance. Anytime they went out all eyes were on her.

After they got married things seemed to go alright for a little while. Like termites nibbling away at the structure, little issues that never seemed to matter began to cause friction. Soon their marriage began to fall apart. She became increasingly frustrated at his little idiosyncrasies. He became more aggravated at her nagging.

"I've had it with you," she yelled at the top of her lungs. "God! You're driving me crazy! I can't seem to do anything right by you," he shouted as he returned fire! "I want a divorce," she said with a growling voice nearly gritting her teeth. he stood in shock never really expecting this from her, but unwilling to relent or to compromise he responded, "Fine! Anything is better than putting up with you!" He stormed out of the room slamming every door and punching the wall in the hallway as he left.

Scenarios play out like this constantly throughout America and around the world. seemingly tiny situations that seem insignificant eventually add up causing devastation and destruction of marital relationships. Once happy couples are now bitter enemies over things that have caused irritation and offense. What causes these things to be to happen? This is a question I get asked all the time. The truth is I was not even sure how to answer this question; but I have seen this scenario play out even in my own relationship with my wife of thirty-plus years.

The word offense comes from a word which means to "off end" someone. whenever we say something or do something that in flicks hurt and pain emotionally and mentally and even spiritually on someone that we love they are thrown off the track they were on. There are three Leading causes that can create offenses and cause irritability in marital relationships.

#1 Disregard for our spouse.

Mike and Janice are good examples of this exact point. Mike is constantly working to provide for the family. He works sometimes endless hours and when he's home he's often exhausted and tired. Asking him questions regarding the home seemed to be something that causes him constant frustration. Yet, Janice doesn't want to bother him so she makes decisions without consideration of how it may impact Mike. Although Janice is planning and trying to make the best home for her, Mike and the children she disregards her spouse altogether.

When asked why she does it she often responds that Mike is usually tired or too busy to ask. If you ask Mike he'll tell you that Janice will do whatever she wants regardless of how he feels or what he says so he says nothing at all.

3 Don't be selfish; don't try to impress others. Be humble, thinking of others as better than yourselves. 4 Don't look out only for your own interests, but take an interest in others, too." Philippians 2:3-4

Disregard for your spouse often looks like you're caring for someone else but in essence are taking selfish actions. Someone who is disregarding their spouse will often look out for their own interests. It's a sense of self preservation. Often it stems from an early development of trauma that could have happened somewhere in their life. As a result, they bring it in to the relationship like old furniture.

The only way to offset this in your spouse is life is to go through scenarios and practices that were contrary to that internal instinct to lookout selfishly for yourself. Practiced habits where you write down your spouse's interests and their opinions in your discussion. If a decision must be made, then you're able to review your spouse's opinions and interests and put them above your own. Often the instinct will be to go with your decision and to justify that your choice is better or right. Unless something is life threatening or going to drain the bank account that it's not worth the fight. The point is to develop a new habit that breaks the grip of the old one.

#2 Devaluing are spouses' opinion

So, encourage each other and build each other up, just as you are already doing. 1 Thessalonians 5:11

We are told to encourage others in the bible. The word encourage means to put courage in. To discourage someone means or implies to take courage away or take courage out. When we devalue someone, we are causing that person to feel less than or worthless.

Look at the birds. They don't plant or harvest or store food in barns, for your heavenly Father feeds them. And aren't you far more valuable to him than they are? Matthew 6:26

If God who is all powerful values, you and your spouse more than the birds of the field who are we to take away from their worth. Instead of taking away we must put worth into them. Studies have shown that words that are demeaning and mean in nature actually steal a person's sense of worth and changes their mental status into one of instability easily provoking emotional and mental trauma.

Your words carry power and can cause a person to take to heart what we say. When we are easily irritated it can become easy to say things that are destructive and demeaning. We never consider the value of our words. When someone you love says things that are devaluing it can promote feelings of worthlessness.

The best course of action is to is to be careful with our words. In times when it can be easy to spit words of poison out, we forget that our words can pierce a soul and a heart. Not talking is not okay. We must be willing to talk things out but choosing how we say things can mean the difference between life and death. Using words like "You always" or "you will never" are condemning words and accusative and cause your partner to feel belittled. Also, these types of words are not correct in nature. When considered in context these words imply that your partner or spouse has a daily, intentional habit of doing what you are accusing them of.

#3 Creating feelings of insignificance

Sometimes causing our spouse to feel insignificant can create feelings of instability. When someone is left to feel insignificant, they feel makes them feel unimportant or small. This often is done when we put other things as a priority above them. Children are important, yet they grow, they get married, they move out and build their own lives. When all that has passed our spouses have been left to feel left out. Statistics have shown that men are more often left out and made to feel insignificant than women.

Overall, these actions can cause offenses in our marriage relationships. The last thing we want is to offend or be offended. Because of this, we try to avoid confrontation. We hide from difficult situations that involve potentially offending our spouses.

So how do we fix this?

As iron sharpens iron, so a friend sharpens a friend. Proverbs 27:17

Proverbs 27:17 - Iron sharpens Iron

Often couples that are experiencing this have not created enough fluidity in their relationship. Fluidity is another way of saying intimacy and communication that creates a intimacy. When there is a constant flow of communication between husband and wife even in the smallest things it breathes and atmosphere for truth and honesty. It's through that truth and honesty that they can keep each other sharpened. What is the best way for a couple to hone their relational skills? By communication. What is the best way for a husband and wife to develop deep rooted intimacy? Passionate well-developed communication.

What makes it hard for a couple to develop and to maintain the fluidity in their relationship is win one or both are harboring deeply seated offenses. It can cause one or both to fly off the handle with accusations and suspicions. It is essential for both, to maintain a well-balanced flow.

The Bible says in Proverbs 14:17 – "A quick tempered person does foolish things." it's easy to fly off the handle and speak without understanding the full weight of information. It's easy to allow preconceived arguments to direct our actions in anger. An angry person is harder to deal with when they are irrational and not listening totally. That is why it is essential for communication.

I once read a book about communication. I wish I could remember the name of the book. It was over 20 years ago. The theme of the book was to teach you how to listen more carefully in communication. James 1:19 Says, "Quick to listen, slow to speak and slow to anger." I believe this is a confirmation of what this book was trying to relate to me and now I am relating this information to you through the book you are now reading.

Offenses are often avoided when you can discipline

yourself to listen. When you listen carefully and ask questions openly and honestly you are creating a pathway to better understanding. When you have better understanding you are able to avoid emotional blowups.

If you want to develop a healthy relationship where your love is large, then create defenses against offenses.

CHAPTER 6 DISCUSSION QUESTIONS

1. Can we discuss any instances where either of us felt the need to defend ourselves from an offense within our relationship? How did these situations make us feel?

2. How do we perceive forgiveness in the context of our relationship? Do we view it as a necessary step towards healing, or does it have a different meaning for each of us?

3. Can you share a time when you found it hard to forgive me for an offense? How did you handle these feelings and what could we have done differently?

4. How can we ensure that when we feel offended, we communicate this in a respectful and constructive way, rather than resorting to defensive behavior?

5. What steps can we take to foster a more forgiving atmosphere in our relationship? How can we support each other in this process?

6. How can we create a safe space to discuss offenses and work towards forgiveness? How can we ensure that both of us feel heard and understood in these discussions?

7. How can we better understand each other's feelings and reactions when an offense occurs, and use this understanding to promote forgiveness and healing?

LARGE LOVE DOES NOT KEEP SCORE

Jesus knew what they were thinking, so he asked them, "Why do you have such evil thoughts in your hearts? Matthew 9:4

Win Matthew pinned this book he was describing Jesus' ability to discerned the hearts of men. The Pharisees were looking for a reason to kill Jesus. They were testing him in every area to see if they could catch him. Jesus continued to astound them with his wisdom. He knew that they were plotting evil in their hearts toward him.

In marriage it can become easy to create or to hold onto records of wrongdoing. If you are always looking for something wrong to point out about your spouse you will always find what you're looking for, even if you must fabricate it. Don't misunderstand me. If there is a wrong being done to you by your spouse, cheating, abuse, manipulation, etc. Those things are reasons to point out to your spouse: if they're willing to hear it.

But what about when we become dissatisfied in our relationship to our husband or wife? What if, any little thing they do we hold it against them.

Janet was dissatisfied in her marriage. She had grown bored with Mike. Mike was easygoing, sometimes to a fault. Mike often forgot their anniversary and her birthday. There were days that he even forgotten the few basic things she sent him to the store to purchase.

"My God," She yelled with disdain toward him. "How could you be so dumb? I mean, I give you one simple list of things; deodorant, toothpaste, milk end you forgot the deodorant," She screamed in a tone that seemed to Pierce his ears. "I don't know," he responded with his head looking to the ground Like a little boy being scolded by his mom. "I guess I had things from work on my mind and I've been pretty tired lately," he continued.

"Tired! Tired? You wouldn't be so tired if you weren't on your Dang phone so late at night," she continued like a barrage of armor piercing bullets. "I don't know why I even married you, I could have married Peter instead and maybe wouldn't have all this headache," she said with her teeth almost grinding.

With a hopeless look on his face Mike responded

back, "maybe you should have. Honestly, nothing that I do seems to please you." "It's not about pleasing me, it's about doing things with common sense," she spat back now with her face staring out the window.

A week later Mike comes home early from work. Seeing Janet's cell phone on the kitchen counter he couldn't help himself. Out of curiosity he had to check and see if she could be texting anybody else. Much to his surprise he was devastated to see an ongoing conversation with Peter, His college rival.

He and Peter head start out friends. Even though Mike lived in the dorm across the hall from Peter, they always made time to hang out and play pool at the student lounge. Mike and peter we're both sophomores when Janet who is a freshman. Mike noticed her right away from across the science class. Janet would smile back with a almost bashful grin and looked down and then look away. Mike was bitten.

Much to mikes surprise, after going home for a funeral one week, he discovered that Peter and Janet, we're seeing each other. This made his blood boil because Peter new how he felt about her. "Relax, there's other fish in the sea. Janet is my girlfriend now," Peter said with a hint of arrogance as if to rub it in Mike's face. "How could you? You knew how I felt about her," said Mike. "Bro, she never saw you that way and you never made a move," Peter said grinning like a Cheshire cat.

Fast forward one year and Peter breaks Janet's heart. Who was there to pick up the pieces but Mike. she had cried on his shoulder when Peter told her it wasn't going to work. As a result, Mike saw an opportunity to be there to comfort her in her time of need and she so him as someone stable and reliable. She fell in love with who she felt he could be. He fell in love with her for who she was.

Now, Janet is texting Peter. The conversation was not about his well-being or even about his family or his marriage. They were threads of complaints about Mike and how she regretted being married to him. What was worse was Peter made no effort in the thread of conversation and texts to push her away and back to Mike.

he continued to scroll through what seemed like page after page of text messages filled with complaints about their marriage and about him. The more he read the heavier his heart felt. It was as if someone had tide and anvil to his heart and to his soul.

When she arrived an hour later Mike was seething with rage and feelings of betrayal. Not even waiting for her to set the groceries down he erupted like a volcano who had been dormant for years. The volcanic ash of words came exploding out of his mouth. "I found this conversation on your phone that you're having with Peter!" "What are you talking about?" She asked. holding up her phone almost to her face he said with a strong tone, "this! This right here! All these texts are about me and us. These are things you should have told me and not him," He responded now shouting.

he continued his rant, "how could you? After how he treated you in college. Knowing how I feel about him. do you honestly want to run back to that?" She responds now with the tone of hate in her voice, "he says he regrets what he did to me and wishes he could make it up to me." "Make it up to you? What does that even mean?" He asks. "I don't know," she replies, "but it's definitely not what's happening here."

With tears starting to build in his eyes Mike could not take the pressure anymore and stormed out the door. Janet went to bed with her face to the wall. When Mike arrived home well after midnight he chose to sleep on the couch.

The next two weeks we're brutal. Every little thing Janet did Mike would point it out. He began to hold count of the way she brushed her teeth or combed her hair. If she didn't do the dishes after dinner, he would make sure she knew as she missed up. Janet was reaching a boiling point but was willing to change if she could get Mike to forgive her.

"Do you regret what you did," asked the counselor. "Yes," she responded with tears in her eyes. "I regret that I allowed myself to be swayed by the one person who betrayed me in college." At first Mike scoffed at her comment. His heart was so full of anguish and feelings of betrayal. "Mike, do you feel that you can forgive Janet for what she did," The counselor asked him. "It's not a matter of forgiving what she did. I must get past the wounds that have been inflicted over the years because I didn't measure up to him. Now I want her to feel how I did all those years," Mike replied.

"She has been mean to me for as long as we have been married," He continued. "I just want her to know what it feels like to be treated as a second."

Janet was now fighting the tears as they cascaded down her face like a waterfall. "I'm so sorry that I treated you the way I did," She cried barely getting the words out of her mouth. Through stammering lips and words almost undiscernible she said, "I don't regret marrying you. I love you and want to be with you and no one else. I allowed things I saw in you and my conversation with him to cloud my view of who you really are." Mike was now looking intently at her. He had shifted his body language from resistance to listening. Her words were now beginning to pierce through the walls he had built up around his heart.

Can you please forgive me? I know I'm a work in progress and you have been the only one that has had the patience to walk with me through all of it. A moment of silence I filled the room. The counselor did not even dare to move for fear that he would disrupt the process of healing taking place.

Looking down and fumbling with his hands although softly spoken were the words, "I forgive you; will you forgive me?" They both stare at each other in the eyes for what seemed like an hour. This was a stare not of positioning or dominance but of soul searching. "Yes, I forgive you too." After the counseling session the car was quiet the whole ride home. Not because neither had anything to say, but because neither knew what to say next.

As she walked into the bedroom to change her clothes, Mike came up behind her and held her. He could feel her body relax in his arms. Something she had not done for years. She felt her very soul shift as the warmth of his body adjusted to hers. She knew everything would be okay.

There are cases like this all the time all over the world of married couples and even dating couples that become; Distracted, disillusioned, discouraged and even depressed in their relationships. As a result, they began to look for faults that they had once overlooked. Little quirks that made them fall in love are now the splinter underneath the skin of their finger. Or the pebble in their shoe.

When your spouse falls do you find that you get excited to put them in their place? perhaps you don't celebrate they're stumbling's, but maybe you still look for faults. Remember we talked about holding no record of wrongs. Our view of our spouse should be Like God does toward us. His mercies are new every morning and our view of our spouse should be one where we allow them the grace to begin again.

How Do We Keep From Holding No Records

When refer to "holding no record of wrong," you're not referring to being forgetful or forgetting the wrong that has been done. The ability to forget wrongs done; that have caused tremendous pain and inflicted wounds so deep that it will require years of processing and counseling, seems almost impossible. No one person can forget wrongs, except for the Lord. Little minor things can be overlooked, but over time they become the bricks that build a stronghold of resentment and trauma.

Instead, we are saying, that we are choosing not to remember the behavior that has inflicted trauma.

Not remembering requires making a choice. Just like forgiveness requires a choice. Despite knowing the attitude and behavior and offensiveness of our spouse we make a choice to walk in love and forgiveness.

Yes, it is true that it is easier said than done, however, practicing love and forgiveness makes perfect.

CHAPTER 7 DISCUSSION QUESTONS

1. Can we discuss any instances where either of us felt like we were keeping score in our relationship? How did these situations make us feel?

2. How do we define 'keeping score' within the context of our relationship? Do we perceive it as a sign of imbalance or something else?

3. Can you share a time when you felt like I was keeping score? How did it impact you and our relationship?

4. How can we ensure that we maintain a balance in our relationship without resorting to keeping score? What strategies can we adopt?

5. In what ways can we improve our communication to express our needs and expectations without making the other feel like we're keeping track of who does what?

6. How can we create a safe space to discuss instances where we've felt like the other was keeping score, and work towards understanding and resolution?

7. How can we better understand each other's contributions to the relationship and express appreciation without keeping score?

LOVE JOYFULLY CELEBRATES THE TRUTH

Love joyfully celebrates honesty and finds no delight in what is wrong. 1 Corinthians 13:6 TPT

Jason and Leah had struggled for more than five years since his affair. Both were raised in church. Both believed in God. Yet, when the affair happened Leah felt a sense of superiority over her husband. This caused constant conflict between them both.

"I just want to get back to normal," Jack said. "Normal? You have fallen way below normal, buddy. You have a long way to go to be normal," she responded back with a tone of arrogance. "What do you mean by that," Jack asked. "Because you messed up you have a long way to go to earn my love and I'm pretty sure God is not happy with you either," Leah responded.

"Look, I know I had an affair, and I am sorry it ever happened, but I can't move forward if all you ever do is make me feel like I'm never going to get past it," he responded with his head hanging down.

"Leah, you need to look at how you would want Jack to respond if the shoe were on the other foot," said the counselor. "If you had done what Jack did would you want him to respond in the same way, or would you want him to kick you emotionally and verbally," the counselor continued. "I guess that I have been so angry and him that I wanted him to feel the pain that I have been feeling that I didn't realize that I could demonstrating love instead of judgement," Lead replied.

"Jack," Lead said as she turned to her husband with a look of compassion, "would you forgive me for holding your emotions and healing hostage?" "Yes, God yes," he answered as he reached out to embrace her and she him.

Some many couples are experiencing this type of emotional, mental and personal feelings. These feelings keep us from releasing our spouses from the chains that keep them hostage. It is not until they release verbally and emotionally their husband or wife that they can truly embrace truth.

When believers demonstrate love for one another, they do not demonstrate superior morality by taking pleasure in another's fall. Injustice, regardless of the form it takes, cannot be enjoyed by love. However, love does the opposite. The one and only truth can be found only through the relationship believers have with Jesus Christ (John 14:6). It is important that those who love do not become tainted with evil. It is instead imperative that they constantly search for truth, that they desire the truth to prevail, that they protect the truth, and that they proclaim the truth whenever possible.

How We Demonstrate Love

Because love is a verb, we are motivated and required to demonstrate it toward others. We cannot say that we know God and not demonstrate love toward fellow man. Despite their behavior or moral failures; despite their disappointing choices and behavior, love is expressed, not in words, but in action. Not because of the gifts we give or the flowers we buy or the sexual intimacy we express, but because of the moral character of love.

That is why this book is so important to your understanding of how large love really is. As you read through 1 Corinthians 13:4-8 you see how love is truly demonstrated. Because the very nature of God is love, meaning He is incapable of not showing love. We know that He is our leading example of how love should be toward others. (see 1 John 4)

That leads us to the question. How do we demonstrate love toward our spouse or toward others? The simple answer is through God. The long answer is more complex.

Our flesh finds it hard to love someone who has let us down or consistently disappoints us by their attitudes or behavior. Through God it becomes easier. Notice I didn't say easy. The reason is because without some struggle in love we lose the ability to grow in love. We grow in love as we learn to love those who are appear to be unlovable.

Sincere Joy Springs From Deep Love

Marriage, as a sacred union, is a profound manifestation of deep love between two individuals. This deep love shared between spouses often gives birth to sincere joy, a concept that is well supported in the Bible.

The Bible provides numerous insights into the relationship between love and joy in marriage. The Song of Solomon, a biblical book that celebrates marital love, is replete with verses that depict joy springing from love. For instance, Song of Solomon 1:4 says, "We rejoice and delight in you; we will praise your love more than wine."

This verse beautifully encapsulates the joy that arises from the deep love between spouses.

In the New Testament, Ephesians 5:25 advises, "Husbands, love your wives, just as Christ loved the church and gave himself up for her." This verse not only instructs husbands to love their wives deeply but also compares this love to the sacrificial love of Christ. The joy that springs from such a profound love is sincere and fulfilling, much like the joy we derive from our relationship with God.

The Bible also highlights the joy that comes from the love and mutual respect between a husband and wife. Proverbs 5:18 states, "May your fountain be blessed, and may you rejoice in the wife of your youth." This verse suggests that the joy experienced in marriage is a blessing, a gift that springs from the well of deep love.

1 Corinthians 13:4-7, often read during wedding ceremonies, describes love as patient, kind, and devoid of envy or pride. This passage suggests that love nurtures joy by fostering an environment of understanding, respect, and selflessness. When spouses love each other in this way, their marriage becomes a source of sincere joy.

The Bible provides a profound understanding of how sincere joy springs from deep love in the context of marriage. The verses from the Song of Solomon, Ephesians, Proverbs, and 1 Corinthians all illustrate that the deep love between spouses is a wellspring of sincere joy. This joy is not just a fleeting emotion but a lasting state of happiness and fulfillment that nurtures the marital bond. As such, love and joy become the cornerstones of a successful and blissful marriage, according to biblical teachings.

Love Celebrates Honesty

In a romantic relationship, love and honesty are intertwined in a delicate dance that shapes the strength and depth of the bond between two individuals. Love, in its purest form, not only values but actively celebrates honesty.

Love and honesty share an intrinsic relationship, where one often catalyzes the other. In the context of a couple's relationship, this connection becomes even more crucial. 1 Corinthians 13:6 (TPT) states, "Love joyfully celebrates honesty and finds no delight in what is wrong." This verse encapsulates the essence of the relationship between love and honesty, indicating that true love thrives in an environment of transparency and truth.

The celebration of honesty in love manifests in various ways within a couple's relationship. Firstly, honesty fosters trust, an essential component of love. When partners are honest with each other, they build a strong foundation of trust. This trust, in turn, deepens their love, creating a nurturing environment where love can grow and flourish.

Secondly, honesty promotes open and effective communication, another vital aspect of a couple's relationship. When partners are honest, they create a safe space for dialogue, allowing for the expression of thoughts, feelings, and concerns. This open communication strengthens the bond of love, fostering empathy, understanding, and mutual respect.

Thirdly, honesty in a couple's relationship leads to authenticity. Authenticity refers to the celebration of one's true self, including strengths, weaknesses, triumphs, and failures. Love that celebrates honesty encourages this authenticity, allowing partners to be true to themselves and each other. This authenticity further strengthens the bond of love, as it fosters a deeper understanding and acceptance of each other.

The Bible provides further insight into this concept. Ephesians 4:15 advises us to "speak the truth in love," emphasizing the importance of honesty in a loving relationship. This verse suggests that honesty should not be harsh or hurtful, but communicated in a loving, compassionate manner. It illustrates how love not only values honesty but also guides the way it should be expressed.

Love celebrates honesty in profound and significant ways within a couple's relationship. Honesty fosters trust, promotes open communication, and encourages authenticity, all crucial for love to thrive. The celebration of honesty in love is not merely about speaking the truth; it is about creating an environment where truthfulness is valued, respected, and encouraged. By celebrating honesty, couples can strengthen their bond and nurture a love that is deep, authentic, and enduring.

Love Finds No Delight In What Is Wrong

The essence of love is often encapsulated in its ability to uphold the virtues of truth, integrity, and righteousness. One of the profound truths about love is that it "finds no delight in what is wrong," a principle that holds significant implications for couples.

The principle that love finds no delight in what is wrong is a cornerstone for healthy and thriving relationships. As stated in 1 Corinthians 13:6 (TPT), "Love joyfully celebrates honesty and finds no delight in what is wrong." This verse encapsulates the essence of love's relationship with righteousness and wrongdoing, indicating that true love thrives in an environment of truth, integrity, and righteousness.

For couples, this principle manifests in various ways. It implies that love does not condone or ignore harmful behaviors or actions. When one partner transgresses against the other, love does not sweep the wrong under the rug. Instead, it confronts the issue with grace and understanding, seeking resolution and growth.

This principle also encourages accountability within the relationship. Love that finds no delight in what is wrong promotes honesty, transparency, and responsibility. It urges couples to own up to their mistakes, apologize sincerely, and make amends. This accountability strengthens the bond between partners and fosters a healthier relationship.

Love that finds no delight in what is wrong guides moral decisions within the relationship. It serves as a moral compass, guiding couples towards actions and decisions that uphold the values of respect, kindness, and fairness. This moral guidance helps to nurture a relationship that is not only loving but also grounded in integrity and righteousness.

The Bible further emphasizes this principle in Romans 12:9, where it instructs, "Love must be sincere. Hate what is evil; cling to what is good." This verse echoes the sentiment that love should not find delight in wrongdoing but should instead cling to righteousness. It serves as a powerful reminder for couples to base their relationship on sincere love that rejects evil and embraces goodness.

The principle that love finds no delight in what is wrong holds significant implications for couples. It encourages confrontation of harmful behaviors, promotes accountability, and guides moral decisions within the relationship. By upholding this principle, couples can foster a relationship that is not only loving but also grounded in righteousness and integrity. Ultimately, love that finds no delight in what is wrong paves the way for a relationship that is healthy, thriving, and deeply fulfilling.

How Love And Joy Work Together

The verse subtly highlights the interplay between love and joy. It suggests that love and joy are not mutually exclusive but are intertwined. Love fuels joy, especially when it involves celebrating honesty and upholding righteousness. This interplay suggests that maintaining honesty and righteousness in our relationships can lead to a joyful experience of love.

Love and joy are two fundamental emotions that significantly shape our lives and relationships. In the context of a couple's relationship, the interplay between love and joy becomes even more profound.

The relationship between love and joy is a symbiotic one, where each emotion fuels and amplifies the other. Love, in its essence, is a deep affection and care for another person, while joy is a state of happiness and fulfillment. When these two emotions interplay in a couple's relationship, they create a vibrant and fulfilling bond that enhances the overall relationship.

Love often serves as a source of joy in a relationship. When individuals love each other, they derive happiness from each other's company, from shared experiences, and from the mutual care and respect they offer each other. This joy is evident in everyday interactions, shared laughter, mutual achievements, and even in the comfort found in each other during challenging times. As stated in Proverbs 17:22, "A joyful heart is good medicine," implying that the joy derived from love can have a healing and uplifting effect.

Joy can also strengthen and deepen love in a relationship. Shared moments of happiness and joy can bring couples closer, fostering a deeper bond of love. Joyful experiences create shared memories and can help to build a strong foundation of love. In the Bible, Nehemiah 8:10 states, "The joy of the Lord is your strength." This verse, while not directly about romantic love, suggests that joy can provide strength, which can be interpreted as strengthening the bond of love between couples.

Lastly, the interplay of love and joy creates a positive cycle in a relationship. Love leads to joy, and this joy, in turn, deepens love, leading to more joy. This positive cycle fosters a healthy, vibrant, and fulfilling relationship. As stated in 1 Corinthians 13:6, "Love... rejoices with the truth." This verse implies that love finds joy in honesty and righteousness, further highlighting the interplay of love and joy.

The interplay of love and joy plays a significant role in a couple's relationship. These emotions influence and enhance each other, creating a vibrant and fulfilling bond. Love serves as a source of joy, and this joy, in turn, deepens and strengthens love. By understanding and nurturing this interplay, couples can foster a relationship that is not only loving and joyful but also deeply fulfilling and enriching.

CHAPTER 8 DISCUSSION QUESTIONS

1. Can we discuss moments in our relationship where we felt our honesty led to a celebration of truth? How did these moments make us feel?

2. How do we perceive the concept of 'celebrating truth and honesty' within the context of our relationship? Are our views aligned or do they differ?

3. Can you share a time when our honesty allowed us to celebrate a truth, either about ourselves, each other, or our relationship? How did that impact us?

4. How can we ensure that our relationship continues to celebrate truth and honesty? What practices or behaviors can we adopt to encourage this?

5. In what ways can we improve our communication to express our truths honestly and celebrate them?

6. How can we create a safe space to discuss our truths and celebrate them together, even when they might be challenging or difficult?

7. How can we better understand and appreciate each other's honesty, and find joy in celebrating the truths we share as part of our bond?

LOVE IS A SAFE PLACE

Love is a safe place of shelter, for it never stops believing the best for others. 1 Corinthians 13:7a

"I just don't feel safe around you John," Christina replied, "you're careless and reckless, and you don't know how to be discreet about our personal lives."

John and Christina had been married for five years, and during those five years it seemed more turbulent than blissful. Christina loved John and was willing to work on things, but he had to be more mindful of creating a safe place for her. John was used to living life one day to the next, never planning anything and just going with the flow. When it came to driving, John had gotten in more accidents in one year than Christina had her entire 32 years of life. Above all, John would hang out with his friends and complain to them about everything Christina said or did. Sometimes it wasn't complaining, it was seeking advice.

"I don't feel like I'm doing anything wrong, I'm somewhat confused that I don't create a safe place for you," John rebutted. Christina shot back, "John, I should feel comfortable coming to you about things that I feel and things that I'm thinking and know that you will keep them between you and me. It's more than just protecting me physically, I need you to protect me emotionally, mentally, and even spiritually."

John sat blank faced, looking straight at Christina as if his mind was somewhere else; as if his mind was no longer in the conversation, but he was there he was just processing. "When was the last time we went to church?" Christina asked. "I don't know, we went on Easter, I think," he answered with a bewildered tone. "I want more in my life than church once or twice a year. I mean, I could go to church on my own, but I want you to take me as my husband."

It was as if a light bulb had been turned on in John's mind. Strong feelings of failure began to overwhelm him as he realized he had failed his duties as a husband in loving his wife. He had become acclimated and comfortable because she never said anything. Sure, there were times when she would make things uncomfortable and stonewall him, but she never said much, she just waited for him to step into his place.

After a while, women will only endure so much, and then they will speak out how they feel. If they feel they are not being heard, they will seek out elsewhere, and that will make them feel safe.

One of the most essential needs of women is security. It goes above physical protection and transcends emotional, mental, relational, and spiritual protection. While the husband's need is acceptance and honor, women and even men need to know that love can be a safe place. No one person should feel as if they cannot come and be transparent and not judged. They should know that they can come to their spouse and will not be criticized or belittled.

Love must be a place where a husband or wife knows that their spouse believes the best for them. When they confide in them, they know their secrets will be safe. When they confess to them, they know they will be heard and forgiven.

Why Is Love A Safe Place?

When life has driven you over the edge and the

children have pushed you beyond the threshold of emotion, it's there that you want to escape to a secluded place to regain your control before you say or do something that you will regret. This is a safe place. A place where you can regain your control before you do something that you could never take back.

As in any relationship, sometimes your spouse will push your buttons in some way that makes you want to lose your mind. It could start with something that said was hurtful, or your spouse forgot your birthday, even though you've been together for long enough to remember. Having a safe place in your spouse means you could go to them for emotional, mental, personal, spiritual, and relational support.

From the ends of the earth, I cry to you for help when my heart is overwhelmed. Lead me to the towering rock of safety, for you are my safe refuge, a fortress where my enemies cannot reach me. Let me live forever in your sanctuary, safe beneath the shelter of your wings! Psalms 61:2-4

The psalmist David refers to God as his safe place. He says, "I cry to you when my heart is overwhelmed." You or your spouse should have a safe place in each other. You should feel comfortable to come and cry when your heart is overwhelmed. Imagine how your husband would feel if he came to you looking for emotional support, and you tell him, "Stop crying! Be a man!" He would no longer feel that you were a safe place for him, that he could come to you for emotional support or even for encouragement. Not every man is an emotional creature. Some have yet to tap into their emotional statuses as men and learn to be empathetic toward their spouses. Some women can be overly emotional, especially when that time of month comes. She should be able to come to her husband even in her emotional state and confide in him, and he would be understanding and compassionate toward her.

It is important for love to be a refuge in a relationship. Without it, both husband and wife become two people existing in a relationship without connection. Security in your love should be anchored to the agreement that your love is safe, and that you will guard, nurture, and uphold with honor your spouse.

How Is Love A Safe Place?

Love is a place called home. It is a place where you can unwind, a place of warmth and comfort. As a pastor, they have an unpredictable schedule. There are days when I will have long counseling sessions. Planning sessions with my staff or church clean up days. Sometimes I'm called on to do funerals and weddings. I am exhausted when I get home mentally and emotionally, and sometimes even spiritually. I look forward to coming home to the love of my spouse. She is my safe place. Truth be told, I have not always allowed myself to confide in her. There have been times in our marriage where I kept to myself and allowed my emotions to take control. I stopped opening up and confessing my struggles and thoughts to her. It wasn't anything she had done. It was how I viewed love. My wife is a "gitter" done person. When I come to her with a problem, her mind automatically goes into fix it mode. All I want is for her to hear me and understand.

Love is being treated with respect and honesty. Without respect and honesty, the walls of your refuge began to crumble. It is impossible to build a strong relationship without respect and honesty. Love is no longer safe when there is no respect.

Respect his honor, which is given both mutually and because of position towards someone. Often respect is earned because of a person's character. Respect is like credit given to someone who has applied for credit. Initially, it is given, and how it is managed determines if more respect is aborted. The way husbands show respect to their wives is by honoring their wife with honesty and truth. There is no place in love for lies! When dishonesty occurs in a relationship, it breaks down the connection between husband and wife. Lies begin to smokescreen what little truth is evident, and cause one or the other spouse to question everything their partner does.

Transparency is key to love being a safe place. Honesty in marriage is what rolls out the red carpet of respect. Transparency means to be seen through. It means being open with no hidden agendas. Sometimes, one might feel guarded with their spouse. Perhaps trauma in your past has caused you to guard yourself in your relationship with your partner. Without transparency, there can be no honesty in a relationship. Being transparent means being vulnerable. It requires being open and honest about who you are, and willing to reveal secrets, even shameful ones, with the one that you love and trust the most.

Love includes understanding and compromise. There can be no compromise without understanding. Without understanding and compromise, relation-ships are struggling and gasping for air to live. If you've ever had your head held under water at some point, your mind decides it needs air if you're going to live. If neither spouse can understand, then compromise cannot be negotiated.

Understanding is the ability to receive knowledge and information and apply it. It's when you become sympathetically aware of other people's feelings, and you allow yourself to become tolerant and forgiving. Times couples lose communication when one or both spouses refuse to come to understand the other person's feelings and thoughts.

Compromise is the ability to enter an agreement that will help settle tension as both spouses make concessions. When a husband and wife get married, they make concessions to live together as husband and wife. Each of them brings habits and practices that they have learned over life. Some of those habits and behaviors may cause conflict and tension in their relationship at some point in their life. umm

When you are loved, you are honored and allowed to be who you are. Not being allowed to be who you are in your relationship is like being smothered. It takes the air out of your relationship. Within every relationship, we should be given the freedom to be who we are; to be the person with whom our spouses fell in love. They fell in love with your spontaneity. Their humor enamored us. They fell in love with our talents for the arts. We fell in love with their generosity. When those things become stifled, it's as if the wind was taken out of the sails. Wind in sails helps propel a boat forward toward its destination. When the wind is gone, so is the momentum.

We must return to the reasons why we fell in love

with our spouse. What was it that caused you to become drawn like a magnet to them? These reasons become thin and weak over time, and eventually become what starts to easily irritate us. Perhaps we expect our partner to mature past the things we first loved about them. Maybe we expect them to grow into someone different and stop being who they were when we fell in love with them. Yes, we should expect our partners and ourselves to grow into someone more than who we first met. Yet, we should allow reflections of them to poke through as a way to remind us of the person we love.

When we downgrade ourselves to please our spouses, it creates an unhealthy relationship. It creates an environment for resentment and retaliation. It provokes emotional outbursts that eventually turn into full-on volcanic eruptions that take out everything in its path. In love, you should not have to change who you are to stay in the relationship. Although relationships evolve, and we as people evolve in our character, our knowledge and patterns of behavior. In love, you do not degrade yourself for the sake of pleasing someone else.

Instead, those who love must value each other. Philippians 2:3-4 says, *"Don't be selfish; don't try to impress others. Be humble, thinking of others as better than yourselves. Don't look out only for your own interests, but take an interest in others, too."* In other words, we show value by placing others above ourselves. We show worth by preferring others' interests over our own. In marriage, humility goes farther than selfishness. The verse says *"Don't look out only for your own interests, but take an interest in others, too."* When was the last time you showed interest in what your spouse wanted to do? What was the last time you put them above yourself? My wife is a master at this behavior. To say she's my hero is an understatement. Words could not describe my admiration for her ability to put others' interests above her own. She is the most selfless person I know.

When you love large, there's no need to be selfish, because loving large means being selfless.

When Love Stops Being Safe, What Then?

One of the greatest needs of women today is security. It's the ability to be safe and feel safe in a relationship without having to worry. Most women are worriers. Don't get me wrong, I know some men who are worriers too. While most men thrive on praise, honor, and treats, women prosper and feel good when their men make them feel good. I'm not talking about sexual gratification, I'm talking about safety. This is not just a need for women, but also for men. We must feel safe, but what happens when love stops being safe what then?

There are certain things that create toxicity in relationships that render them unsafe. Things like manipulation, jealousy, and control, just to name a few. But also, dishonesty, infidelity and disloyalty can be equally toxic. What does a person do when the atmosphere of love is no longer there, and now the storm clouds of danger begin to loom over their heads? There are ongoing discussion groups and theological debates regarding when it's time to bail. Everyone wants their relationship to work. No one gets married, and while they're walking down the aisle in their heart, they're saying, "I hope this marriage fails." We all start believing and wanting our relationships to thrive. We all fall in love and want to grow old with the person we are in love with. Sometimes, however, things don't always work the way we want them to.

In my 30 plus years of ministry, I have seen trauma invade marriage relationships, causing them to break down over time like the grain of sand under the millstone. I have watched as unresolved issues fester and become like an infected scab on the heart of a marriage once strong. Is it right to pull the plug? Is it right to call it quits? Does God honor my life and the life of my partner if we go our separate ways? The key to this book is not to incite divorce or even separation, but reconciliation and restoration. The love I'm talking about in this book is the character of God toward us, his children, and should be our character toward our spouses and others.

When the relationship becomes infected with the poison of bitterness and unforgiveness, it may be best to find peace during separation while actively pursuing restoration and reconciliation. When the relationship becomes so toxic, but neither spouse is willing to try, it may seem like it's time to throw in the towel. I believe we have been called to the ministry of reconciliation, and that before quitting, we try loving.

When your love becomes unsafe, it's wise to push the pause button. Not for the purpose of pursuing other relationships or seeking divorce. You're pushing the pause button to reflect and seek counsel from someone who will point you toward the answer in a biblical and godly way. Unless there is physical abuse in your home, and you are in danger, there's no reason for you to move out and create additional stress and trauma to your marriage and to your children and spouse. I don't like the idea of legal separations or even trial separations. Pushing pause means you stop conversation about the issues that have created the stress in your relationship, and actively pursue wise counsel so that you can discuss the issues at hand in a wise way.

How To Create A Shelter Of Love

To create a shelter of love, as with any structure, a foundation must be set. Shelters require foundation, otherwise they become unstable and are subject to crumble when the winds of testing come. If you cannot build off a foundation, your structure will not be sound. Jesus said in Matthew 7:24-25:

[24] *"Anyone who listens to my teaching and follows it is wise, like a person who builds a house on solid rock.* [25] *Though the rain comes in torrents and the floodwaters rise, and the winds beat against that house, it won't collapse because it is built on bedrock."*

In this parable, Jesus points out the importance of foundation and how it leads to a solid structure for any home. In this illustration, Jesus refers to a building your home upon him. He is the solid rock. I have cancelled marriages that one or the other partner is not a Christian. Already set on a rocky foundation. It's obvious the couple loves each other and wants to be together, but their differing opinions cause them to become unstable. Having your home established upon Jesus Christ may not make it perfect, and you will have struggles and arguments along the way, but it will become easier because Christ is our strength.

When building a shelter of love, one must also build the structure upon that foundation. You must have a vision and plan for how you will accomplish this. This requires three things 1) open and honest dialogue or communication. It doesn't have to be pretty, but it has to be honest and transparent. Without it, your structure will be unstable and not able to create a sound environment for your marriage to thrive. 2) Trust is also essential. Without trust, a couple cannot survive. Dishonesty and lies will decapitate your relationship, causing it to implode into a heap of distrust questions and suspicion. Keeping open communication about everything will help the marriage thrive, heal, and create an environment of trust. If I can trust you with my pearls, I know you won't trample them. 3) Transparency is also important. Transparency is a facet of honesty and truthfulness. Transparency, as I mentioned, requires vulnerability. You must be willing to be open about your feelings and understanding your partner's feelings, and willing to work to bring healing.

No shelter is complete without power. What brings light to your life? What causes you to become excited? What provokes you to become a bundle of joy? For some couples, it's date night. For other couples, it's regular intimacy in the bedroom. For other couples, it may be praying together. Once you discover what brings life to your life, actively work hard to bring that to your partner. Remembering special memories, birthdays, days meaningful or times meaningful in your partner's mind is crucial to bring power to your shelter. Forgetting it's like getting the power cut off in your home. We live in an electronic world, and all of our electronics depend on the power in our home. Once the power is cut, those gadgets only last so long before they die too. In the same way, you cut the power in your shelter of love, and little things that were there before will eventually die, and so will your relationship.

You can't have shelter without a roof over your head. I'm not talking about a physical roof, but a figurative one. This shelter of love depends on a strong foundation, a sound structure, power to bring light and warmth, but also on your cover. If you're a man and reading this, it is essential to get your family and your marriage into God's house. When a man is not undercover, he is not covered. When a man steps out from under God and under God's house, he cannot guarantee security and safety to his family. If you're a woman and reading this, realize the importance of raising your children in God's house. You can substitute little things in your life that will eventually take the place of God in your marriage and home, but you will soon find that keeping God at the center of your marriage is crucial for thriving and having a successful relationship.

Make time to worship together. Find moments where you can be together in worship, allowing God's presence to consume you and cover you. We seem more vulnerable and open to receive after worshiping God. There's something about his presence that causes us to open and feel safe. Make every opportunity to worship in God's house, pray together, worship together. And when you do, you will have created a shelter of love.

CHAPTER 9 DISCUSSION QUESTIONS

1. Can we discuss times in our relationship when we've felt that our love for each other provided a safe place and believed the best for each other? How did these moments make us feel?

2. How do we perceive the concept that 'love is a safe place and never stops believing the best for others' within the context of our relationship? Are our views aligned or do they differ?

3. Can you share a time when our love provided a safe place and believed the best for each other, especially during a challenging time? How did that impact us?

4. How can we ensure that our love continues to provide a safe place and keeps believing the best for each other? What practices or behaviors can we adopt to encourage this?

5. In what ways can we improve our communication to express our belief in the best for each other, and how can we make our love a safe place?

6. How can we create a safe space to discuss our challenges and still believe the best for each other, even when times are tough?

7. How can we better understand and appreciate each

other's needs for safety and belief in the best, and find ways to provide that in our love for each other?

LOVE NEVER GIVES UP

Love never takes failure as defeat, for it never gives up. 1 Corinthians 13:7b

"Do you love your husband," the counselor asked. Raquel hesitated a moment before responding, "I think," she pauses to choose her words carefully then she continued, "I think I have fallen out of love with Marcus." The look on Marcus' face was as if someone had just thrown cold water on him. "How can you say that?" he asked with a tone of bewilderment. Raquel sat for almost two minutes before responding, tears welling up in her eyes, "you have put me through so much these last 12 years. I think I grew tired of your mistakes and you're apologies."

Marcus sat in the counselors office with a blank stare. His emotions had completely shut off now. then he stands up grabs his jacket and thanks the counselor for his time. As he walks to the door to leave the counselor calls his name, "Marcus, please sit down we're not finished." "Well, apparently my marriage is," Marcus says as he turns and looks at Raquel with anger and her in his eyes. It was as if he couldn't choose between one or the other. he is now in a position of protection guarding himself from further hurt. The counselor turns to Raquel and asks, "Raquel, when do you feel that you lost feelings for Marcus?"

She turns from looking at the counselor to looking at Marcus and tears began to well up in her eyes, "I think I got tired of the lies. Lies upon lies. Marcus, I hurt so bad on the inside that the pain drowns out what love I have. I'm afraid to love you and continue to be hurt by the lies you tell." Marcus stoops down to his knees and then leans against the wall in almost a near fetal position. The truth becomes like a boulder on his shoulders too heavy to carry and too Big to face. Raquel continues, "I know you said you're sorry and you apologized. I think I lost count of how many times I heard, 'I'm sorry' and then you did it again."

By now, tears are streaming down Marcus's face like a waterfall. His chest was trembling as if a silent earthquake was happening on the inside. His face begins to contort at the visible sign of trying to fight his emotions. Raquel rises from her seat and walks across the room and kneels next to her husband. "I, I think, I'm afraid to say I'm sorry again," Marcus says through a quivering voice almost near a whisper and then he continues, "how can we move forward when I know how you feel? when I know how I made you feel."

She turns and looks at the counselor and says, "this is the first time I have seen him this vulnerable. This is what I need." She leans in and kisses him on the top of his head, and he turns and looks at her with a tear-stained face. He rises off his knees and pulls her up to her feet with his hands holding her shoulders he says, "I will never give up on us."

thousands of couples just like Marcus and Raquel suffer in silence afraid to face the pain and the truth of confrontation. Out of self-preservation they lock down their emotions like a prison not daring to allow their feelings any room.

What Does It Mean That Love Never Gives Up?

What does it mean that love never gives up? In order to answer this question, let us examine how God loves us and how his love never fails.

The very nature of God is revealed in several ways. It

is revealed in his love toward us by his sacrifice in Jesus Christ. It is revealed to us through his patience toward us when we are stubborn. The Bible says that there is a depth with height and breadth to God's love. Since God is everlasting and his patience toward us is everlasting his love toward us is never ending.

Love never gives up because our love for each other is manifest in the character of God within us. I know we are human, and our patients is confined to our human ability to endure mistreatment, betrayal, subjugation, and misdeeds. Our finite minds cannot perceive someone who has hurt us, betrayed us, cheated on us, lied to us and mistreated us. We are confined by the boundaries that are set by our traumatic experiences issued upon us by people we trusted and loved.

As a form of self-preservation, and self-protection we shut down the areas of our mind and our emotions to preserve ourselves from further pain. We convince ourselves that love doesn't feel this way therefore we no longer love. We tell ourselves this to keep ourselves grounded behind a wall of denial. The truth is that love does hurt and endures many highs as well as many lows.

When we examine our love compared to that of God's, we find that we fall short every time. God's love toward us is never ending even when we fall short of reciprocating his love back to him. How many times have we given our love to something else and not to God? How many times have we placed priority of our lives and our happiness above honoring and pleasing Him? Yet he continues to love us and endures the pain of betrayal, rejection and at times hate from us his children.

I know you must think that this kind of love is different from spousal or matrimonial love but in essence it's the same thing. Love is love. What differentiates love of God from love of one another is his divinity and our humanity. Another thing that differentiates divine love from human love are the classifications of love. For example, agape love is godly brotherly love that is shared between Christian men and women. It is the expression of God toward one another any respectful and loving way. Phileo love is neighborly love. It is the love we have for people in our community that have and share the same commonality as us. Eros love is the love a husband and wife shared with one another. It is a love that is both agape and Phileo combined while being different because it is expressed through romance and intimacy.

No one wakes up in the morning and says, "Gee I hope my spouse hurts me today!" By human nature when pain comes, especially emotional and mental duress we run from what is causing that hurt and pain. We develop a sheltering mentality and build a fortress in our heart and mind to protect us from those that have hurt us. When we've allowed ourselves to become closed in and highly guarded it can feel like our love has ceased to be.

Love that never gives up is a love their endures every trial and every betrayal. I'm not saying that if you are in an abusive relationship that you should stay there and continue to endure psychological emotional and even spiritual damage. Instead when you love someone you will continue to love them by confronting them and challenging them to change.

God's love never ceases. In other words God never stops loving us. When we continue in our reckless behavior and refused to listen and refused to change he becomes silent and even at times he distances himself from us until we realize that he is no longer there and we come returning to him. Notice I never said that he stops loving us. Even in his absence he loves us. The people who are awaiting judgment who have passed away in their sin he loves them too. He does not want to send them to hell and even in his sending them to their eternal judgment he loves them still.

It is possible to love someone but for sanity's sake and for mental health one must distance themselves from some one who continues to be destructive. In these times our love does not fail. In our absence our love never ceases. Should our spouse continue in destructive self-sabotaging behavior our love never ends. Though our heart breaks for their choices our love never ends.

What If I No Longer Love My Spouse?

I have been asked this question a number of times throughout my years of ministry two couples. Although I will address more of this in the next chapter allow me to do a brief overview.

I believe that when couples love each other they never stop. If you no longer love your spouse my belief is that it's because you never loved them to begin with. When you love someone deeply and passionately you never stop loving them. Even if they separate from you and file for divorce and move on with their lives a part of us always remains in love with the person we married.

Some couples get married because they are infatuated with their spouse. When they begin dating they fall in love with the concept of a spouse. Many times men marry women believing that they will have sex every day whenever they want it. Women merry men believing that they will have continual protection, constant cuddling and affirmation. During the dating process we go through the process of courting our potential mate. We begin to demonstrate behaviors, attitudes and actions that our future spouse should expect to receive once we are married. However and we become married we stop the behavior.

men have A conquering mentality. It is innate inside every man to conquer. From the beginning of time when God created men to now we are created to show and demonstrate alpha behavior. We lose weight, we workout, we dress nice and Comer hair. We take our girl to eat at the best places. We spend every waking moment entertaining our future wives. We make her feel safe. We make her laugh. But once we say I do real life begins.

Women have been trained and instructed as homemakers and mothers. As little girls they play with dolls imagining their knight in shining armor or their Ken doll to come and sweep them off their feet. They laugh at jokes that are not funny. They endure Little glimmers of control. Like the men they lose weight, they may even cook they dress nice and portray which should be expected after marriage.

With most women in their mind they continue the process that they began during the courtship. But with the men once the woman has been conquered and we take her to our castle we no longer need to conquer her. We stopped taking her out to eat. We no longer dress the same way we did while we were dating. We no longer feel the need to impress the one whom we have married.

As time moves on and behaviors become worse we feel

as though love has died. We have based it upon a false premise and an illusion of expectation. When those are no longer there it can feel as though love has died.

The good news is that love, true love, never fails. When you love someone deeply and passionately your love will continue even in the worst of times. When we have God in our hearts to love our spouse who at some point feels unlovable. We can look at them through eyes of compassion and say genuinely that we love our spouse.

We may not tolerate their behavior. Their attitude might exasperate us and push us to the brink of exploding into an emotional tirade. Their betrayal may cause us to want to run and hide but when you love someone love never gives up. Love never ceases to see the best in people. Because love sees people through the eyes of God and not through our own human weaknesses.

The reason God can love us unconditionally, patiently and without end is because He sees in us what we fail to see in ourselves and in others. It's only when we see others through His eyes we will understand why this verse says that love never quits.

CHAPTER 10 DISCUSSION QUESTIONS

1. Can we discuss times in our relationship when we've felt our love was tested but never quit? How did these moments make us feel?

2. How do we perceive the concept that 'love never quits' within the context of our relationship? Are our views aligned or do they differ?

3. Can you share a time when our love was challenged, but we didn't give up on each other or our relationship? How did that impact us?

4. How can we ensure that our love continues to be resilient and never quits, regardless of the challenges we face? What practices or behaviors can we adopt to encourage this?

5. In what ways can we improve our communication to express our commitment to each other and our determination that our love will never quit?

6. How can we create a safe space to discuss our challenges and reinforce our commitment to each other, even when times are tough?

7. How can we better understand and appreciate each other's needs for reassurance and commitment, and find

ways to show that our love will never quit?

NEVER QUIT!

*Never give up, for that is just the place and
time that the tide will turn.*

Harriet Beecher Stowe

Marriage is hard work. It is a house that never ceases to need repair, maintenance and upgrading. It requires our full attention and constant concentration. Without our consistent effort our marriages will begin to slip into the sea of thousands of divorces that could have made it.

No one ever promised that marriage would be easy. No one ever said that marriage would be all love and no confrontation. In fact, marriage is better described in Ecclesiastes 4:9-12 *"Two are better than one, because they have a good reward for their labor. For if they fall, one will lift up his companion. But woe to him who is alone when he falls, for he has no one to help him up. Again, if two lie down together, they will keep warm; But how can one be warm alone? Though one may be overpowered by another, two can withstand him. And a threefold cord is not quickly broken."*

This passage describes two comrades in arms. To people in battle. Marriage is like this. A battle. Not against one another, but alongside of one another. Where two fight side by side.

He says in verse 9, *"Two are better than one, because they have a good reward for their labor."* This verse implies that the two are laboring together. It directs our attention to the idea that they are building or working toward something. In marriage we are building, something. We are building a home, a life, a family, and a future. These should be our goals in our relationship. All other "goals" should be secondary or complimentary toward the five directives.

I think that marriages get into trouble when we take our eyes off the goals and begin to shift the priorities toward more self-seeking outcomes. We stop building a future and start reconstructing our present. We stop building a family when we change our perspectives toward more selfish values. When we work together and are in agreement toward the values we want to see we will see success and more peace in our home.

Next, all wise Solomon says in verse 10, *"For if they fall, one will lift up his companion. But woe to him who is alone when he falls, for he has no one to help him up."* Solomon implies that a fall will happen, and it will happen to them both. *"If they fall"* he says. In marriage when one falls, we all fall. When the husband makes a mistake, he takes the home with him. When the wife falls, she destroys more than just herself. Their fall initiates a generational trauma that becomes a seed in the minds of their children.

The good news is that if "they" fall, one can lift the other. If "they" stumble one is there for the other to pick them up. In other words, they are to be there for each other. All too often couples push each other away to suffer in silence. This doesn't ignore the idea that they are both not hurt or crushed by the weight of the fall. More so that the one who didn't cause the fall is strong enough to pull the other up. It is far easier to kick the other person while they are down. To belittle them for them for their ability to not remain standing.

This reminds me of the verse in Galatians 6:1 (Amplified):

BRETHREN, IF any person is overtaken in misconduct or sin of any sort, you who are spiritual [who are responsive to and controlled by the Spirit] should set him right and restore and reinstate him, without any sense of superiority and with all gentleness, keeping an attentive eye on yourself, lest you should be tempted also.

When one falls the stronger one should restore the

spouse in a spirit of gentleness and love. True the fall often causes pain toward the partner. In times like this it is hard to forgive or overlook the pain. In fact, the pain causes us to want to lash out at our husband or wife and say, "How could you be so stupid?! How could you have not been more attentive?!"

What do we say to the wife whose husband cheated on her? How do you respond to the husband whose wife has had a moral failure? When we are in a deep relationship with God the pain is felt, but the compassion is our motivator. The deep love of Christ who is the restorer of everything broken.

No one wants to be alone when they are with their loved one. Yet in times of failure and falling alone is often the course of punishment prescribed by others including the ones we trust the most. Solomon reminds us, *"But woe to him who is alone when he falls, For he has no one to help him up."*

Marriage is a constant investment of time, attention and effort from both husband and wife. It requires sacrifice and selflessness. When we find our mate, our life partner, our spouse we expect them to be a support to us and vice versa. However, we never expect to be a companion or an Allie. Solomon says in Ecclesiastes 4:12:

Though one may be overpowered by another, two can

withstand him. And a threefold cord is not quickly broken.

This verse implies that the two will come under some attack. Spiritual attacks come after every family for what they represent. They must remain in constant communion and maintain a continual unity of Spirit, mind, and body so that when one is overpowered the other comes along side and creates a power pack. *"There is always strength in numbers,"* Mark Shields When the two (husband and wife) stand together they are a force to be reckoned with. All though outward attacks may come they are able to withstand the attack.

In our thirty plus years of marriage, my wife and I have endured some of the ugliest spiritual battles one could ever think to face. We have fought the enemy of our marriage, Satan, and at times have come to almost being each other's enemy. Yet, I could not think of anyone I would rather have fighting alongside of me than the woman that I fell in love with over thirty years ago.

My wife is a fierce woman of God. I have seen her grow Spiritually over the years. I have seen her shed tears of sorrow and tears of joy. She has confronted me out love more times than I care to admit. She has come along side of me to call me out of my dark places. When I think of Ecclesiastes 4:9-12 I think of her.

What Happens When You Quit?

We rarely think of what would happens should we quit. The pressure of the moment squeezes us to the point of wanting to pop. We cannot stand to be confronted or to confront. It is exhausting to endure reckless and careless behavior from a person we love.

As of 2023 from 35% to 50% of marriages end in divorce. One or both spouses call it quits. Often due to irreconcilable differences. Out of one hundred couples thirty-five to fifty of them will end up quitting. Rather than standing up for marriage the two walk out.

Quitting is easier than sticking it out. Please read what I am about to say clearly. There is no way that you should stay in an abusive relationship or one with continued unrepented infidelity. For the betterment of your mental health, it is better to move forward. Moving forward is not quitting, it is moving on without the one who refuses to grow with you. Even if you love someone you never stop loving them. You only decide to love them from a distance.

Quitting however creates a pattern in our psyche that programs us for leaving whatever is too difficult to fix. If you have always been a quitter, you can look back on your life and realize the pattern of quitting that you have created over your entire life. When you love someone, quitting is not an option.

"Love never ends," is how the New King James translation describes it. Real love, true love never ends. In other words, the perfect love of God never quits. It knows no end nor how to quit loving those it loves.

Incredible thing, God's love. He loves the sinner, while sending them to an eternal hell. Love is not tolerating wrong behavior, but in love punishing wrong after numerous pleadings for change. The bible tells me that we should have this same love.

"Dear friends, let us love one another, because love is from God, and everyone who loves has been born of God and knows God. The one who does not love does not know God, because God is love. God's love was revealed among us in this way: God sent his one and only Son into the world so that we might live through him. Love consists in this: not that we loved God, but that he loved us and sent his Son to be the atoning sacrifice for our sins. Dear friends, if God loved us in this way, we also must love one another." (1 John 4:7–11, CSB)

John, the beloved, starts by saying that we should love one another because love is from God. Then, he highlights it by saying that anyone who loves is born of God. When you are born again (born of God) you have the nature of God in you, and it should be naturally instinctive to love others. In marriage we love one another romantically, but also through the love of God.

To say, "I fell out of love with you," or, "I don't love you anymore," is to say your love has failed or quit. "I have quit loving you," is what our minds are telling us. Really what it means is we have blocked loving the other person because we don't want to be hurt or feel the emotion of hurt and disappointment. So rather than allow our hearts to sense the pain that comes from loving someone so much, we block it.

Love never quits, really. It's always there. Even in times of separation and divorce. "What about times when couples have been divorced and marry someone else?" you may ask. Yes, even then love is still present. If two people truly love each other the love will always be there even if they move on to another relationship. They will never love the other person the way they loved at first but love never quits.

For our love to remain strong we must pursue the love of Christ. With that love comes hurt and disappointment. We must allow our emotions to be hurt. We will have our egos bruised, but the true love that never quits will help to shape our relationship with our husband or wife.

When we think of love, we imagine a Hollywood romance move type of love. Everything just falls into place and just happens. Even the love scenes are perfect. All of that is smoke and mirrors. That is all staged to look its best from different angles. Real love happens at home, in the kitchen, in the bedroom, in the car in places where no one sees. It is developed first in the heart of each person and then expressed toward one another.

True love, that never quits is developed over time. Today marriage is treated as a disposable item. Something that you through away when its broken or no longer working the way you want. We get uncomfortable with exchange or confrontation by our spouses and want to walk away. We encounter disloyalty and regret our vows. True love is as we have revealed in this book.

Love is patient and kind; love does not envy or boast; it is not arrogant or rude. It does not insist on its own way; it is not irritable or resentful; it does not rejoice at wrongdoing but rejoices with the truth. 1 Corinthians 13:4–8a (ESV)

You see these elderly couples that have been married for over fifty years. They have weathered the storms of life. They have experienced loss, heartbreak, disappointment and even lack and have lived through it. I'm sure they wanted to give up and quit, but instead they kept going.

My friend or friends as you read this book don't quit. Don't throw in the towel on your marriage. Realize that LOVE IS LARGE. Love is never ending. God's love helps us to cast out all fear and love deeply. True love enables us to love so much deeper. That is why love hurts at times. It is the reason we experience love from a different view when we are in love with someone. The deeper your love goes the more profound your love can become.

Think of it as an endless cavern of tunnels for your to explore. Take your time and journey. Mine the nuggets of wisdom that someday you'll hand down to your children. Work through areas that seem impossible and do it all, together.

Other books by Maurice Chavez

Build A Better Marriage

Build a Better Marriage (Spanish)

Managing Your Marriage In Ministry

Communication -Ebook

Reign

Reign (Spanish)

Fresh Anointing

www.ingramcontent.com/pod-product-compliance
Lightning Source LLC
Chambersburg PA
CBHW071446090426
42737CB00011B/1794